DISCOVERING *the* GREAT *I Am*

ONE WOMAN'S JOURNEY TO FIND GOD

SHERRY GRIFFITH, BS, MSW, LCSW

Copyright © 2022 Sherry Griffith, BS, MSW, LCSW.

All rights reserved. No part of this book may be reproduced, stored, or transmitted by any means—whether auditory, graphic, mechanical, or electronic—without written permission of both publisher and author, except in the case of brief excerpts used in critical articles and reviews. Unauthorized reproduction of any part of this work is illegal and is punishable by law.

ISBN: 979-8-88640-211-7 (sc)
ISBN: 979-8-88640-212-4 (hc)
ISBN: 979-8-88640-213-1 (e)

Because of the dynamic nature of the Internet, any web addresses or links contained in this book may have changed since publication and may no longer be valid. The views expressed in this work are solely those of the author and do not necessarily reflect the views of the publisher, and the publisher hereby disclaims any responsibility for them.

One Galleria Blvd., Suite 1900, Metairie, LA 70001
1-888-421-2397

New discoveries in recent years are overturning the last 150 years of scientific thinking. The old story that's been embedded in our lives for generations is no longer valid and no longer serves us in healthy ways. We have the rare opportunity to rid ourselves of this old story and create a new story that offers tremendous self-healing, new sustainable solutions and stronger family and community bonds.

> In order to create this new story, we must first do what our ancestors did before science and technology prevailed in our world. We have to tune into our heart-intelligence.
> —Gregg Braden
> ***Resilience From The Heart*** (Hay House 2015)

Contents

Preface vii
Stuff Before Chapter One x
The Backdrop xxi

Part One: The Story 1

Chapter 1   The Setting 3
Chapter 2   Adolescence 15
Chapter 3   Early Adulthood 23
Chapter 4   The Gift 38
Chapter 5   Cancer 56
Chapter 6   Adventures In Consciousness 61

Part Two: "I Am" 67

Chapter 7   Adventures in Consciousness 73
Chapter 8   Embrasing the Gifts 89

Part Three: Recipe for Conscious Manifestation 143

Afterthought 165
Definitions 167

Preface

January 2014. My ex-husband and I had been divorced for 14 years, bumping into each other at family gatherings for the kids and grandkids. I texted him with a reminder to send his annual check for his share of the amount of the money that we were depositing into the grandkid's accounts. He responded he would. The next day he texted me saying he didn't see any reason why the two of us should ever communicate again.

I was dumbfounded. What had changed? The discomfort of seeing each other at family events had long been resolved, or so I thought, and we had always communicated about the kids and grandkids when necessary. I felt hurt and offended. The old feelings that I thought I had exorcised, the ones of anger and resentment, overwhelmed me. I responded with a terrible text. The second I pushed the send button, I regretted it. That wasn't me and hadn't been me for a very long time.

In an instant of enlightenment, what I had believed was the truth about my life I realized was a fiction of my own making, a story I'd told myself and everyone else about who I was. With certainty, I knew he and I had agreed to play roles for each other to facilitate our learning and everything had always been exactly perfect. I'd chosen my experience with him, and I was as much a part of the designing of that shared experience as he was. On an intellectual level, I'd known this. But I felt it at a deeper level where intellect and emotion blend into one knowing.

I forgave him. I forgave myself. Then I realized there was nothing to forgive.

I was flooded with insight and began writing for clarification. Then I began to write a book. I became totally immersed in a process begun by that incident. I felt myself accelerating so fast that soon I couldn't focus on writing the book and stopped writing it at Chapter 6. My book slid to the back shelf of my mind.

Months later someone from a publishing company where I had expressed interest called. "Where's your book?" She tried to back me into a finish date. I dodged and made excuses about being busy. She let me know she wasn't buying it. What I didn't tell her, what I hadn't clearly seen myself, was I was still writing it every day in my journal. After a lifetime of wanting to know answers to the big questions of who I was, why we are here, and whether or not there is a God, I was having experiences that were closing in on some answers.

This book is in three parts: first a description of my story as I told it before my enlightenment, the second was my process of finding God, and the third part is a recipe for stepping outside one's story and into possibilities. I've analyzed my experience to clarify the steps I took in the hope that it will help others in their own process of becoming. It will be another thought map into conscious manifestation, like the ones I found and followed. There are many, but all lead to becoming masters of manifestation through channeling the God Consciousness.

I am discovering what I knew as a small child about my connection to what I called God. It's with a lot of insecurity and more than a little fear that I have gone through with exposing myself by writing this book. Is this real, or am I full of shit? Is what I'm writing valuable to anyone else? Sometimes I don't know. When I questioned this, I received the answer, *"It is what you asked for, Sherry. The universe is delivering."*

I approach this project with open expectation, happy to have envisioned where I want to go and knowing that the process of my expanding consciousness is continuing. It is never finished. My intention is to raise my own vibration and to help others do the same with the larger goal of saving our species from certain extinction unless we heal the earth through healing ourselves.

I am so full of gratitude for this earth, for my life, my family, my partner, my career, my home, my privileges, all of the real life "teachers" I've had, and all of my experiences.

I can't wait to see what comes next.

Sherry Griffith

(Fractal S: When I first published this book, I used a pen name at the publishers request due to the personal nature of my story. I have chosen to republish using my own name with a different publisher. However, Fractal S is significant as it further illustrates the fractal nature of consciousness, which is the theme of this book: that we all contain the entirety of the ALL THAT IS consciousness within us.)

The revolution of scientific understanding suggests that from our personal health and relationships to global war and peace, the reality of our lives is nothing more and nothing less than our "belief waves" shaping the quantum stuff that everything is made from. It's all related to what we accept about our world, our capabilities, our limits, and ourselves.

Excerpted from pages x to xii of Spontaneous Healing of Belief, by Gregg Braden. Copyright © 2008 (Hay House).

Stuff Before Chapter One

Consider how fast the legality of gay marriage became a reality once it had gained a critical mass of supporters. It started slowly, then state laws against it began to topple. Those who supported it and worked for it were stunned as court after court countrywide declared the laws against gay marriage unconstitutional. I can proudly state that my home state was one of the first to challenge the laws of an old way of thinking. A deluge of people took advantage of same sex marriage before the window temporarily closed again while the state government contested the federal judge's ruling. Changing the status quo is like trying to put leggings on an active toddler. There is a lot of wailing and thrashing about.

So much more change is coming: the right to have access to the means to end one's own life with dignity, the right to experiment with consciousness using (now declared illegal) substances, the recognition of all of mankind and of all creation as being part of one organism and one consciousness, the decision by mankind to heal the earth before she eliminates the bulk of us in order to regain her balance, the possibility of worldwide peace and respect for the divinity of everyone.

At times, it seems impossible that these things could happen. Instantaneous and worldwide communication personally involves us in every tragic event and deviant thing that happens anywhere. It feeds us our reality, and we tend to let that happen with very few questions about who is in control and why the information provided to the masses is what it is. If one digs deeper than what is presented on mainstream media it becomes clear that a lot of important information is conspicuously missing and there are some entities, well concealed, but very rich and powerful, who are managing common awareness in such a way that they are benefiting financially and shuttling resources their way. This may be something we will see change when a critical mass of people challenges the validity of the story presented to us. This is precisely what appears to be happening in the US and in every part of the world. People are rising up against the political and social status quo and revolution is in the air. Social media is the new way of structuring our reality according to our interests and beliefs. Its potential to provoke change is amazing. It's also unpredictable and can be suspect.

I want to say something about "critical mass". There is a story called The Hundredth Monkey. As I understand it, some scientists were observing primates on an island in New Guiney. Each day they would throw sweet potatoes onto the sandy beach for the primates. I don't know what behavior they were studying. But at some point, the scientist noticed that the matriarch of the group walked out into the ocean and rinsed off her sweet potato before eating it.

"Ok", I hear you say. "What is so interesting about that? Even lower primates probably don't like getting sand between their teeth." But the scientists noticed that the primates in that singular group on that particular island all started to wash their sweet potatoes off in the ocean before eating them.

"Ok", I hear you say again. "We all know primates can imitate and learn from experience. That's basic behavioral learning, isn't it?" Now comes the startling part, the part that is seen over and over again in situations where a small thing becomes generalized to the larger mass. It is reported that without any direct connection with this group, monkeys all over the local islands began to walk into the ocean to rinse off their sweet potato before eating it.

On some higher level of consciousness there appears to be communication which happens when there are enough individuals to tip the balance just enough to move the whole mass. It doesn't have to be anywhere near a majority, just enough to cause movement…a critical mass. This explains how our society changed concerning gay marriage and the surprising switch in government policy and social mainstream attitudes.

This is the beginning. As critical mass builds, attitudes will change, establishments will be modified or collapse making way for new ones. It is entirely up to us to choose what will replace them. What many of us have been missing is that personal change is the foundation of social change in the shared story of our species. A critical mass is required to tip the balance in favor of peace, fairness, and kindness.

Everyone has their own story which they repeat to themselves and others nonstop. Our brains are continually editing environmental data, arranging it according to our paradigms of belief, assessing it as we evaluate and judge others, ourselves, and events around us. Our stories often conflict with the stories of others who were also "there" at the time. We consider our facts to be true, as do others. When our beliefs don't coincide with theirs, we firmly believe our own version of the story and even hard-core evidence isn't likely to change our minds.

Why is this? How many times have you been told that things didn't really happen the way you remember them? How many times have you told someone else they only remember what they want to remember, while believing you don't do this yourself? Are we trying to be dishonest about things? Not normally. We tend to REALLY believe that everything happened the way we remember and that we are justified in proclaiming that our perspective is the right one. Yet, the evidence shows that everyone has their own version of "the truth" when it comes to the recollection of the same event or situations.

The main reason for the fluidity and faultiness of memory is that we incorporate our perception of events as viewed through the lens of our preconceived beliefs about ourselves, others, and the world. These beliefs are well established and solidified by about the age of 7 or 8 when we have developed a core system of beliefs that form the structure of our lives. They tell us who we are. They tell us what the world is. Everyone does this. This is how personality is shaped and molded from the structure of our genetics, assimilated into our unique dispositions, and acted upon by environmental forces. It is how we attribute meaning to our lives, how we connect with others, how we function. Although it is a natural process, it isn't without inherent problems.

We develop the story of self, believe it, allow it to direct us, and form our personal reality. It limits us if we don't understand this, leaving us to revolve around in the fairytale of ourselves indefinitely. As we identify our story and develop the ability to step outside of it, we become conscious of the freedom to create the life we want. In my case, it led to the discovery of who I am, who we all are, and what existence is all about.

Many philosophers through the ages have discovered this before me. This is nothing new. This knowledge is part of indigenous cultures across the world. My favorite philosopher is one Carlos Castaneda wrote about in his books. Don Juan Matis was a Yaqui Indian living in the Sonoran Desert of Mexico who took Castaneda on as an apprentice. He was a brujo, a medicine man who was regarded by many of the locals as crazy. Castaneda has since been accused of making up some of the fantastic material in his books about his apprenticeship. However, the philosophy presented is intact and is the same across many nonwestern cultures.

Don Juan told Carlos he had a violent nature and, therefore, his experiences and his perceptions were flavored by it. This construction of self applies to all of us. At a time when quantum mechanics was an unknown concept to all but physicists, Juan, an uneducated man, was teaching it to Carlos.

Don Juan talked about having no personal history. When I first read this, I interpreted it as him saying we must abandon our relationships in order to delve into non-ordinary reality (consciousness). I felt a similar way about the Buddhist notion of non-attachment. I was wrong in my naïve interpretations. They both are saying that you have to let go of expectations and outcomes, let go of your story so that you can integrate new information. It's about stepping outside of your story and allowing it to change, realizing it isn't anything more than a story. It's about letting go of resistance and just BE-ing.

Once the story is recognized for the fiction that it is, attachment to beliefs, thoughts, emotions, and behaviors no longer becomes the unconscious default. This applies to self-identity and extends to the belief about what reality is and is not. Detaching from the dogma of our lives allows us to explore our consciousness without the confining limitations of what we believe is possible or what is "real". We are free to develop concepts and to create experiences that are outside the norm. Such experiences are the seed of many religions once the doctrine, greed, and need for control is stripped away.

My lifelong quest to find "God" has been the driving force in my life. It has taken the form of self and spiritual exploration with my beloved books as my guides and teachers. I discovered the Divine within me, in everyone, and everything. Even after finding the eminent God within, I still had my story. I just didn't realize that it was only fiction, my fiction. Until…

I've had many spiritual experiences. But the discovery of my story was one of the most profound. My story kept me as contained and controlled as the 50s years did with my mom. It was comfortable living inside that story, not in the sense that it was pleasant, but it was familiar, and I believed in it. I thought I knew who I was and could explain everything in my story so well. After the story was debunked, I allowed myself to stay story-less and to create a new story, a conscious one this time. It is always a work in progress, revising it as I go, now aware that it is just another fiction, but a conscious one.

Every individual has a story built upon a framework of core beliefs. It can be a sad story, a happy one, one filled with frustration, a story of victimization, a story of misfortune, a story of pain, a story of bravery, a story of success… you get the gist. The story is the way a person understands themselves to be within the world. It is ever unfolding, but the basic story line remains the same unless one is willing to view it from an objective perspective.

Read my story with an eye to seeing how my underlying core beliefs provided the framework around which I structured my memories and attributed meanings to my experiences. Remember, this isn't a true story. That one doesn't really exist outside subjective memory and understanding. Although it is not THE TRUTH, there is no other truth. At least not one that can be known. When I realized this, it allowed my story to be changed and molded in a way that changed my life.

You might ask "why would I want to change my story"? If you are entirely happy with your life, yourself, and the state of the world, then you might not want to. If, however, you are experiencing pain, unhappiness, suffering, and lack of fulfillment, you might want to choose change. (Some beliefs may serve you well. But they are still just beliefs, and not "the truth". Knowing this allows you to either choose them or to reject them.) These are the core beliefs we hold, those we have not examined, that are our CORE BELIEFS around which all other beliefs, thoughts, emotions, and behaviors revolve that require change. They form a framework of paradigms that provide meaning to the data we receive from our environment through our physical senses. Information that reinforces our already established beliefs is incorporated and information that contradicts our core beliefs is simply rejected. Repressed and ignored information can be recalled, but only when one is ready to identify their continually rehearsed story.

There is always a core belief that starts with "I am...". Those are potent, prophetic words. <u>This is the belief that defines who we believe we are and what we are capable of doing.</u>

No story is formed in isolation. The family (or the lack of one) is 'ground zero' in story formation. My work as a psychotherapist has provided me with a plethora of information and experience about how we develop the self within it. Understanding the role we embrace in relationships with others is essential in identifying the core belief leading to how we define our **self** in this world.

Functionality in any family system falls along a continuum and has nothing to do with wealth, intelligence, or education. Rather, it is defined by how effective the family is at accepting and emotionally supporting each member with their needs and aspirations. Are the members supported by the family structure, or is their duty to insulate the family from outside eyes and influences? In highly dysfunctional families no new information gets in and none about what is happening in the family gets out. Most families operate somewhere along a continuum.

In a functional family, the members still have problems and issues. They experience the entire range of emotions, the pleasant as well as the unpleasant ones. The family does not insist they behave in a certain way or that they feel a certain way. Rather, the family allows the individual their experiences, although support may vacillate greatly.

The functional family is flexible. Its homeostasis is continually being challenged and (here is the key to functionality) the family changes constantly in the never-ending effort to establish a new homeostasis. So, for example, a member of the family may come out as gay. It may initially cause chaos, pain, denial, conflict, discomfort, shock. However, in a functional family the individual members grow and often a new level of intimacy and effective communication comes about as the system shifts to find a new balance, inclusive of the gay member.

Conversely, in a dysfunctional family the members play specific roles in order to rigidly maintain homeostasis. This "normal" state may be very painful to the individuals involved. In fact, it likely is. However, the established homeostasis is the known, and it is therefore more comfortable than the discomfort that comes with self-exposure and temporary imbalance brought about by change. Individual roles of members exist to keep the family locked into whatever pattern it is in, rather than allowing it to change with the individuals and with outside influence. Secrets are kept from the outside world and even within the family itself.

In a dysfunctional family, the announcement that one of the members is gay may be hidden from a specific member, it might never be mentioned again, or the gay member may be expelled. Speaking about that member may not be allowed. There is frequently a choosing of "sides" by the members of the family as they form coalitions. Communications are carefully measured, and information is often concealed from members of the extended family and outsiders as well. The gay member may be sacrificed to maintain the appearance of the status quo. The family doesn't adapt or change. It simply sits in its rigidity and reeks of emotional death.

Families are not either all functional or all dysfunctional but tend to favor one over the other. Occasionally, a painful or awakening situation will occur that will jolt a family into change bringing about a better level of functioning, one where the members will be supported by the family and not sacrificed for the family homeostasis.

There are a couple of theories which attempt to define the typical roles of family members. The names of the roles are not important, only the function. They are not pure categories and human beings are not just all one thing. Some people fit their roles less rigidly than others. Sometimes roles will combine, and the individual will move from the features of one role to another depending upon what the family structure calls for. Some of the roles are passive, some aggressive; all of them limiting to the individual.

As individuals learn and grow, they can change and recognize the roles they play for the family; they can consciously decide to break out and become more whole. Thankfully, life tends to provoke us through pain and discomfort to do just that.

In all families, individual members seek to have their needs for love, attention, and validation met. When a family is operating in dysfunction these things are meted out in a conditional manner, reinforcing everyone to play their chosen/assigned role. We are validated in some way for functioning as designated, and we participate in the validation of the other family members in their roles. It is an unconscious process and only becomes clear when one can look at their beliefs, behaviors, and the dynamics of their family in an effort to make changes.

Some theories explain that birth order determines the part an individual assumes; and indeed, there seems to be a correlation between birth order and role. Other theories attribute roles more to genetics and disposition, to the dynamics between temperaments that leads to powerful coalitions of certain family members, and to biological influences. It's probably the result of all of these forces. And it is important to realize that the roles we assume are not randomly "assigned". Rather, they are the ones our personalities adapt to. We choose them as much as they choose us. This is an unconscious choice, but one that fits.

I'm presenting my story as an example and a template for helping others move from living unconsciously to manifesting what they want. **The details**

of one's story are only important in that through analysis of them one can identify patterns of thought and behavior which lead to isolating problematic core beliefs. This is an essential step in transforming life from what it has always been to something spectacular. The methods to do this will be covered in depth in the third section of this book.

I can't speak with any real authority about the stories that my parents and siblings have created or what their core beliefs are. I have some observations based upon my interactions with them and may mention them. But again, my observations and conclusions will be based upon my version of our story. I only bring up my siblings and other family members as they contribute to the telling of my old version of it.

I will provide more of a picture of the development of my core beliefs by an in depth look at my parents and their relationship, as this is the root of my family story, and my story in particular. I have based their stories on what they have told me and my experience of them.

I will start by setting the stage for my story and by discussing the roles of my family members as I saw them, focusing primarily on my own. I will use the names of four family roles from a dysfunctional family model which have been proposed: the hero who makes the family look good, the whistle blower (also known as the scapegoat) who is emotionally expressive and considered the "bad kid" due to acting out the family dysfunction, the care taker/peace keeper (enabler) who tries to keep everyone happy, the lost child who metaphorically is marginalized to the fringes of the family and the hero who is responsible and "saves" the family in some way. I will also refer to my siblings in the order that we were born, Numbers one through six. This will simplify things for both me and whomever reads this, as I'm sure I'd have difficulty remembering what name I had given to each one to conceal their identity.

Hopefully, reading about my awakening and following my recipe for conscious manifestation will help others step outside their own stories to join the mass of people determined to change our world for the better. I hope my daughters and grandchildren someday identify their own stories and become conscious story makers. I hope every living person is able to achieve this. My excitement is hardly containable. I feel so hopeful for our species and the world. If I have discovered the truth about my story, and others throughout the world and history have discovered the same about their stories, then anyone can. A critical mass of conscious creators can be formed which can change our world and allow for our species to survive and not have to start over again as archeological history indicates we have done many times before.

There is hope. I have always had hope for mankind but wasn't clear about how humanity's survival could be achieved, and peace could become our experience. Now I believe that if enough people step outside their stories and envision a new one, these dreams can become manifested.

In my quest to find "God" and define who I am, I've discovered that we are all God, fragments of consciousness traveling eternity, manifesting, always creating because that's what consciousness does, what it IS. I have finally found what God says in the Christian Bible. "I am that I am, The Great I AM". There is nothing else to know.

May the God/Goddess we are become consciously manifested in all we do.

Sherry Griffith

When you think, choose carefully the thoughts of things you'd like to be. Thoughts entertained in the minds of (wo)men Become Tomorrow's objectified whims."
Ingrum @ravi.rane

The Backdrop

My name is Sherry Griffith. I am telling my original story the way I told it innumerable times. It was all I knew and what I believed without question. The details are a mix of fantasy and fact, important only in that they nudged me to expose my damaging core belief and exit my story. The telling of it is important in that it can help others identify their own stories and recognize them for what they are …fiction. We have to know our story in order to track down our core beliefs. Once core beliefs blocking our potential have been exposed, we can modify them and eliminate their undesirable effect upon our lives. Manifestation only works to our advantage if we are aware of doing it. Otherwise, we are just living unconsciously and automatically, whining and raging about how bad we have it.

So here goes. (Gulp)

Born in 1950, I got to experience the 50's as things were before the revolution that was ignited in the 60s. Things were kind of Leave It to Beaver-ish. Gender roles were locked in place and people didn't question the validity of what was "normal". Society was rigid and one's place within it was proscribed. It wasn't really the happy time it's been touted to be, "the good old days". But it was predictable.

My mother had to hide her pregnancy or risk being let go from her job. My dad was the bread winner and managed all the money, even though my mother worked the entire time I was growing up. Until I was 13 she rarely drove the family car, which made her quite dependent upon the generosity and inclinations of my father. At the time, this was not unusual.

Throughout my life she talked about how she hated living in a rural area, steeped in religiosity and ordinariness, about how she wanted to be a famous writer like William Faulkner or Flannery O'Connor. She compromised all her goals by allowing my father to have sex with her before they were married.

According to Mom, the intercourse "just happened". She didn't want to do it, said "no", but was coerced and very caught off guard that it did. Could she really have been that naive?

She immediately afterward told him he had to marry her…and fast. They were married two weeks later in a rushed ceremony that culminated in riding to her new home in a tiny town (now almost a ghost town, and not much bigger at that time in 1939) in the back seat of Dad's parent's car, while his mother sat in front with my father. Mom's story goes on from there about how she despised the small town, hated living with my grandparents, finally managed to complete her college Bachelor Degree through correspondence classes, had six children which she says she loved but whom held her back from her aspirations of being a writer of merit, and how she eventually attempted to leave my father to move back to the big city where she had grown up, back to her beloved university.

One day in the second decade of her marriage she packed her bags and told Dad she was taking the Grey Hound to the city and leaving him. She had arranged for an interview with the Board of Education, and they promised her a job if her credentials were in order. Instead of letting her go, he "double crossed" her. Dad said he would drive her; he didn't want her taking the bus. She agreed.

At the Board of Education, he also pulled out his teaching certificate and presented it. Dad and Mom were both teachers, and he was the principal of the elementary school in the small town where I grew up until age 11. It was his love, along with the house he built with his own hands. Leaving them was no small sacrifice on his part, albeit a sacrifice my mother resented him for making. Mom said he blindsided her with this move. So, the entire family, without my two older sisters, moved to the "big city".

In those days, a divorced woman was synonymous with a whore. She was a free woman with illicit sexual urges no longer under the control of a man. It seems the general notion was that such a woman was sensuously wild, which made her all the more attractive. She couldn't be controlled easily. There were very few divorced women in those days. A divorced woman who had been married within the sacred temple of our cultish church was as rare as bloody meat.

The 50s are regarded with nostalgia by many, but I believe they are memorialized that way because few people openly questioned the sanctioned way of life. It was simply the way things were supposed to be. I suspect my parents were not the only ones who were seething and disappointed.

Then came the 60s.

What an exciting and traumatic time that was! Just like now. I sincerely believe that I will live to see amazing things in the very near future, such as impossible to imagine (for me) advancements in technology, changes in medicine which will incorporate self-healing, the real power of the mind, understanding the multiple dimensions of DNA, a rewriting of the origins of our species that will go back hundreds of thousands of years to reveal the origin of our religiously defined Gods, and an open and accepting presence of human and other life from other places in this universe and other dimensions.

These years formed the backdrop of my life story and opened my mind to possibilities. I look back on them with gratitude and fondness.

Part One

THE STORY

Chapter 1

THE SETTING

My childhood was a secure one. I knew my parents would take care of me, and I felt loved. This was my experience, and I acknowledge that my siblings each have their own childhood experience, their story. I believe the majority of parents do their best, but that parents are often woefully inadequate. Most of us are just good enough.

#1 came along within a year of marriage. I only lived with my oldest sister seven years before she married and moved out of the house. Most of what I remember of her and what I know of her consists of events that happened after that time. And due to her breaking off completely with my parents when I was eleven, I never really knew her very well personally. Who she was is now is mostly hearsay. She died at 76.

In 1962, she appeared at our house and announced to my parents that she wanted nothing to do with them...ever again. That included them not seeing her two-year-old son whom I adored. That's how things went until over two decades later when #1's husband died of cancer in his 40's and he asked on his death bed that she reconnect with my parents and heal things. She made an attempt, but a reconnection never fully happened.

I know of her rather than knowing her. As a kid, #1 was the hero in the way that mattered in my family. She was smart and got excellent grades.

According to #2, #1 did her fair share of misbehaving, but it went unnoticed. #2 was born two years after #1.

There were eight years between me and #2. She was my world up until she was banished to a private school at the age of 15. I adored her. She played the role of the scapegoat in our family. She and my father were in what seemed to be continual conflict in the battlefield of my home.

It took me years to recognize that I grew up in a violent home. Doors slammed, there was screaming, yelling, name calling, crying. The crack made by the door when both of their bodies were pressed against it on either side, the slapping, swearing, and feel of chaos and despair were the substance of my home. My father accused #2 of "running with the Indians", which was considered a major transgression. We grew up on an Indian reservation and she had some native friends.

#2 ran away from home at least three times, once with my father's car making it all the way to another state with her much younger friend in tow. She was continually trying to escape my family. She made one significant suicide attempt as well, which went un-noticed by my parents, even after #1 brought it to my mother's attention. It simply wasn't information that the family system could acknowledge. Attending to it would have changed the homeostasis of my family and no one was ready for that. So, it was ignored and only disclosed decades later by #2.

My father also accused #2 of having sex with boys. The irony is that her virginity meant something to my sister, so she managed to avoid the actual act until she met her husband when she was 17. I, on the other hand, had sexual experiences at a younger age than she, and my mother provided me with birth control, but kept this a secret. Secrets and coalitions. The point is that I was much like my older sister in many behavioral respects; I tampered with alcohol and tobacco as she did. But my role was the caretaker, the obedient one, the good girl. My transgressions were either reframed in their meanings or were overlooked.

The biggest behavioral difference between me and #2 was that I was not "sassy" and she was. She could, with her wry humor and sarcasm, cut through my father's ego and provoke a rage, something she now admits she did with regularity. And, of course, my unhappy father blamed and beat up on #2 rather than deal with his own emotional misery. Both of my parents were profoundly unhappy, did not get what they needed, and blamed the other for it. As is typical in battering families, # 2 acted out the dysfunction in their relationship. My father never touched my mother in anger that I know of.

My role brought the duties of peace making and taking responsibility. My parents told me I was a good girl…often. You may be thinking, "So, what's the problem?" It might not seem like such a bad role to play on the surface. But I can assure you it restricts and hinders the development of self-identity, disables creativity and individuality, and imprisons every bit as much as any other family role does. On his death bed, my dad told me he expected me to take care of my mother because I was the one who would. As time went on, I found myself rebelling against it in an effort to shed my role. Being a good girl was synonymous with being obedient. I not only got this message at home, but a huge dose of it came through my religious upbringing. Obedience was preached from the pulpit and highly valued in children of God. We often repeated our dedication to "obedience to the laws and ordinances of the gospel" nearly every week in youth church classes. These began at age four and extended up through the teen years and into the young adult ones as well.

As part of being a good girl, my own needs were secondary to the happiness of others, which meant *their* needs were being met to the best of *my* ability, and I was rewarded and reinforced for it. It became central to my identity and led to sidelining my goals and needs to keep things calm and others happy throughout the rest of my life. I still fight the impulse to stifle my own needs and emotions to keep from rocking the boat. And as always, that was the role that fit my disposition and biological traits.

I was about 8 or 9 when my church had a daddy-daughter date night. The girls in my primary class and their fathers met at the cultural hall in the church, played games, ate, and danced. We spent weeks preparing for it. Every single girl had a dad who planned to be there with her…except me. My dad was working or hunting instead. I forget which. My teacher found a substitute, a man who was in our church and had agreed to be my date. I was sick to my stomach. I felt abandoned. And to make matters worse, he stepped on my foot when we were square dancing, and I was in real pain for the remainder of the night. I believed I was important to my dad, and I was devastated by him not choosing to be there with me. He was also deer hunting on most of my birthdays, as the two fell together during October. It's a little thing, I guess. But it felt a lot like I was unimportant on occasions that were important to me.

Somewhere around 9 or 10 I became the family clown. #4 and I invented a language we called Wi Talk. It was more than a language. It was a performance and we played specific roles. (Imagine that.) I was the goofy one who actually spoke the language. #4 was the only one who could always understand my grunts and garbles. We were often in stitches at our own behavior, and it delighted my mother as well.

I could tell my mother I loved her by Wi talking. I couldn't say it otherwise. Wi talk persisted for several years. It was a way to connect the individuals in the family, particularly #4 and me, where there was no other connection. When she and I weren't Wi talking we had ferocious physical fights. Of course. It was a violent family. Wi talk provided an absurd but more functional way to relate, even though the flavor of it was rooted in the family story of roles and dysfunction.

We moved to the city when I was in the fifth grade…for the second time. My mother started teaching all of us to read when we were four years old. I was four when I started Kindergarten a year early because I was reading. I was a good student all through elementary school. When we moved, she suggested I redo the fifth grade because I would be younger than all of the other kids, because the schools in the city were harder and I would be behind (i.e.: I wouldn't be the smartest kid in the class), and I was more immature than the kids going into the sixth grade. I said ok.

Being brilliant, or at least getting top grades, was THE measure of every member in my family. To that end, my mom decided to have #1 redo a grade and #6 redo kindergarten for the same reasons. Know what is odder? (Or maybe not, once the dynamics of dysfunction are acknowledged.) I did the same thing with my oldest daughter. She redid the sixth grade when we moved to another school district. I used the same reasoning my mother used and didn't even question the logic.

Back to my role. I carried the house key around my neck, and my three siblings and I walked to and from our elementary school in the morning and at lunch time. I was in charge, let all of us in the house, and presided over the distribution of the food for lunch. When we moved to the city #2 felt she either had to move with us and stay mired in the family dysfunction or marry her boyfriend...with whom she had had sex. (The importance of that cannot be understated and was a big reason I married my high school boyfriend.) She chose to escape our home.

After she left, the family system needed a whistle blower, and I was briefly auditioned for the part. One day early after moving to Salt Lake my father and I had an argument and I guess I had become "sassy" with him. He followed me to my bedroom and demanded that I bend over for the ritualistic spanking that was given by him when one of us had somehow violated a family rule or made him angry.

In my family spankings were routine. "Bend over for a spanking" happened often while we were children. When we lived in my hometown there were Weeping Willow trees in our back yard. My father would sometimes break off one of the willows, ceremoniously run his hand up it to strip off the leaves, then use it on our bare legs for a more painful disciplinary experience. A neighbor kid once threw some rocks at me from across the road. I pitched some back and must have hit her. She was a few years younger than I and her angry father told mine about it. I was playing in the back yard when my dad rounded the house, grabbed me by the arm, dragged me to the front yard, and whipped my legs with a willow in front of the neighbor and his daughter. At the time, I had no idea why I was being whipped. It was only after the lashing I was told the reason. I had nearly forgotten the rock throwing incident by then. And I certainly didn't see myself as the only perpetrator of the situation.

This kind of discipline was typical in those days of the 1950s. However, typical isn't always functional or healthy. Such behavior is now viewed as abusive, although I wouldn't describe myself as abused as a child. These situations punctuated my childhood on rare occasion. My siblings will undoubtedly have their own perspectives on our family discipline.

Back to the standoff in my bedroom when I was about 11 years old. When my dad demanded I bend over, I looked my father in the eyes and told him that if he was going to hit me he would have to hit me standing up. He didn't hit me then or ever again. I slid neatly into the caretaker role I was already being groomed to fill; and #4, who was being groomed as well, became the scapegoat.

Again, there was the thumping sound of feet running down the hall toward her bedroom and the sounds of violence.

My father had an angry edge to him. He was the principal of the only elementary school in my hometown. Being a proud man, he retained this identity long after the move to the city. My father also had a caring side, he supported us well, and I never went without a tangible need being met.

Mom was a thwarted writer who felt trapped by husband and children. She wrote a poem once which #2 and I found when we were emptying her house before she moved into a supported living community. It was called "The Habit". It clearly showed resentment of her marriage which she always blamed on my father.

Mom lived her life in her books. Intellect was core to her identify. A few years back I was embarrassed when I visited her in senior living. We were at the dining room table with all the other residents when she announced at the top of her lungs, "I'm smarter than everyone here." Her kind friend, bless her heart, gave me a knowing smile. Mom was thoroughly offended when one of the women there confronted her on her snootiness.

#5 was the Lost Child. My father was so proud when he was born because in a family of girls, he had finally had a boy. He and my father locked horns when he was a teen because he didn't adapt to the role my father had envisioned for him. He wasn't a hunter and fisher like my father. After #4 had managed to get out of the house he moved into her vacated role. The family required a scapegoat. I was married and out of the house as well, so #6 moved into my role. He was a "good boy" with all that implies.

#6 played the hero, the baby and darling of the Family". He had big, beautiful eyes, long eyelashes, and dainty facial features. He managed to have a relationship with my father, a "man to man" relationship. It met my father's needs and expectations of a son, the same ones #5 had rejected.

The crucible of my family story was my parent's relationship. My mother wanted her freedom. My father wanted her love. Neither of them had their needs met. I never saw my parents kiss or be affectionate that I can remember. One of my earliest and happiest memories was when I was about 4. My father was working in the garage, sawing wood. Dad started singing, Ka Ka Ka Katie and my mother joined in. I remember feeling for maybe the only time that my parents liked something about the other. In that golden moment, they were happy. I felt so in love with them. But it is the only memory I have like that. I have fond memories of each of them individually, just not when they were within each other's company.

Ordinarily, my mother was very rejecting of my father. If he touched her, she would pull away with a grimace, and tell him to leave her alone. I witnessed it many times. She hated sex and made that well known. Of course, she did. It had trapped her into having a life she didn't want. Her disdain of sex and the oppressive nature of our church and community defined my own attitudes toward it. Sex was sinful, and it was a good girl's responsibility to prevent it before marriage and succumb to it afterward. It is no wonder that getting married ruined sex for me.

My father started sleeping in the basement on a twin bed pushed up against the cement wall when I was about 6 or 7. Mom occupied the upstairs bedroom and that's where she taught me to read. I would be taken from my bed early in the morning and would lie with her and read out loud a given number of pages every day of my childhood. She did this with all her children, even on vacations, even when there was a death. Even on Christmas! Her drive for academic achievement for herself and her children has been both a blessing and a curse for me and my siblings. It was a force that shaped our identities. With the exception of #1, all of us are college graduates, one has two bachelor's degrees, two of us have master's degrees, and #2 has a PhD.

My mother was not comfortable with emotion, except perhaps disgust. It was directed toward any situation that generated emotion, toward my father, other teachers, other parents, other's kids, relatives, and toward anyone who showed emotion. She hated sentiment. Her role was the martyr of the family, long suffering and self-sacrificing, a role she had played in her family of origin. She was the "good" parent. My dad was the "bad" one.

My father was a mixed bag. He was a good man, and he was a terror. My dad was very overweight. Many psychological theorists talk about dysfunction in an alcoholic family. The family role and dysfunction theories started with those families. Although my father never drank alcohol that I know of, he was addicted to sugar and carbohydrates. Many typical dysfunctions arise in a family when there is addiction of one or more members. It's both a symptom and a cause. My family home had a big chest freezer in the basement that always had several gallons of ice cream in it, along with a spoon in each one. Many times, I saw my father stand at the massive freezer with the lid raised above it. I confess that I engaged in that behavior on occasion myself, standing on something so I could reach the treats and barely able to raise the top of the freezer.

My mother was openly critical of my father's addiction. Once, and this has become one of the shared stories in my family, my mother offered ice cream to everyone after dinner. My father politely refused, as he was trying to lose weight again. She scoffed, "You know you want it". He thumped the table in anger and got some for himself.

My father talks about being an overweight child in some audio tapes he made for us just before he died. He clearly had experienced pain over his weight and the ridicule from the kids at school. However, he only stated, "Well, I guess it didn't hurt me much," after talking about a particularly humiliating time when he was forced to dress in horizontal stripes and dance on a stage next to a very tall young man dressed in vertical stripes. Weight was another one of the shaping forces in my family.

Dad had a crude sense of humor. He would make sexual comments and innuendo which embarrassed the hell out of me. Where my mother hated sex, I observed that my father was always after her for it. He was a voyeur and I caught him spying on me when I was undressed on more than one occasion.

When I was a young adult, my father came to visit me at my apartment. He was 63 and just retired. He said then as he had before, that he was thinking of leaving my mother because of her continual rejection of him. Both cycled through thinking about divorce from time to time. He lamented that he had become impotent. I had tremendous pity for my unloved father. My mother's disdain for him rubbed off on all of us and I think we were surprised after he died to realize he wasn't all bad. Dad was an addict who played a scapegoat in my family, which is likely why he scapegoated some of his children, probably the ones he identified with the most. Disgust (my mother's emotion) and anger (my father's emotion) were acceptable; but other emotions were not.

There was another central theme in my family, and for me it was the biggest force. Religion. My mother's own mother and father were products of polygamy. Both of her parents, particularly her father, hated it. Polygamy was the standard in my church for many years before it was outlawed. Then it went underground. Many members continued to practice it and there have been several groups splinter off from the mainstream church that still do. What many people don't know is that "The Principle" (polygamy) is still a core part of the doctrine and it is in the scriptures of the church that all members who go to the highest kingdom in heaven will practice it in the hereafter as Gods and Goddesses. A man can still marry multiple women in the temple of the church, making their unions celestial, whereas a woman can only marry once.

Growing up within my religion was a unique experience. I only knew one girl until I was 11 years old who was not a member. Everything in life revolved around my church and that community. All our rituals and traditions had the church at the center of them. Children in the church were raised to believe that it was "the one and only true church of God and Jesus Christ", and all other religions were wrong. Only the members who had been baptized into the religion and who made religious covenants, or promises to God, would be eligible for Godhood in the celestial kingdom. All others would be relegated to lower kingdoms and be denied God and Goddess-hood.

My mother always struggled with her faith. She questioned the church doctrine and took issue with some of the practices. She applied her beloved intellect and couldn't help herself when she couldn't find reason for things of a faith-based nature. Mom turned her back on the church from time to time, then turned back to it when she felt the need for spiritual connection. She didn't take her membership in the religion lightly and the family followed her in and out of it repeatedly. My father included.

He was not from church origins. But he wanted Mom to love him so he converted to the church and married her with the sacred covenants when I was a baby. He even got a circumcision to make sex more palatable to her, and because the religion espoused it. It didn't work. Each time Mom left the church, she would take off her church garments, that strange underwear that devout members of the church wear. This is considered to be one of the most egregious sins. Dad would eventually do it too to keep pace with her. (The garments, one piece until recently with a slit in the crotch for toileting and intercourse, symbolize the purity of the individual and the ordinances one takes when making covenants with God. When I was a child, members were told to never take them off except to bathe and have sex. Since then, other exceptions have been made. In the beginning days of the church, members would bathe with them hanging from one limb to never have them completely removed. They now come in two convenient but still unattractive pieces.) The importance of my religion in my home and upbringing cannot be understated.

It is interesting that my mother knew virtually nothing about religions other than the one she was raised in. She was alternately either an active church member or an atheist. Her spirituality was completely framed within either of those two options. She asked me in her later years what I believe. When I told her she literally turned up her nose and made an "ick" sound. "You don't really believe in reincarnation, do you?"

When I was about 13 my mom was reading the existential writers and preparing to exit the church. I started reading them too: Sartre, Camus, and Dostoyevsky. We would have philosophical discussions and I concluded at 15 I was atheist as well. I was also having sex with my boyfriend. It was simply too much for me to sit in my church class and listen to how I was supposed to stay "sweet", while craving sex again as soon as possible. It coincided with the first of my own religious exits.

As a child I had felt a strong spiritual connection to ….whatever it is that is often referred to as "God". I remember lying in the back yard in a sleeping bag and looking at the stars. I became part of them. I talked to God continually. I did it in my mind and I did it out loud. But when I became atheist, I stopped talking. As a result, my intuitions became more blunted. I remained atheist until I was 27 when everything changed.

In addition to Mom teaching me how to be a scholar, she taught me to question authority. Mom was an interesting dichotomy. On the one hand, she was a fierce questioner of authority, and on the other hand she was the epitome of conformity. Fear of being different and of regretting her decisions defined her approach to life. She often said, "I'm afraid" when she was faced with choice or change. The context of this comment was not the issue. What is significant is that this is the way she met the world, and it is what she passed to me. Afraid not to be good, afraid to make a socially unacceptable choice, afraid to break the rules. Mom talked about choices, thought outside the box, then openly disapproved if I made a move to exit the box too far.

My father taught me to manage money and to work hard. He always worked multiple jobs and was famous for squeezing a nickel until the buffalo shit…as my partner now jokingly says of me. It was part of being the responsible one, and it has served me well. I learned to manage money and be disciplined at work. I learned to push through difficulties by using self-restraint. That's a good thing… most of the time. It also led me to deny dynamics in my troubled relationships and led me to tolerate the intolerable. Like anything else, skills can be utilized well or misused.

Summary: supporting core beliefs…

- Intellect is superior to emotion.
- A woman is obligated to have sex when she's married.
- Good girls don't have sex outside of marriage.
- Sex outside marriage is against the rules. Only bad girls like sex.
- Always question the status quo.
- Don't violate the status quo.
- Good girls are OBEDIENT to the rules of the status quo.
- Good girls always are responsible to meet others needs before their own.

CORE BELIEF: I am a good girl.

Chapter 2

ADOLESCENCE

THE REINFORCEMENT OF CORE BELIEFS

I adored #2. She was my world. She and I called each other Penna, which meant friend. We spent hours on her bed listening to KOMA broadcasting out of Oklahoma, a faraway place. I know all the music and lyrics from the 50s and early 60s because of this. The Everly Brothers and Brenda Lee were my favorites. We played cards ("scards" in our lingo) for hours singing along.

But she and my father were at war.

Then suddenly she was gone. My parents sent her to a private school in a remote location. She now says that saved her life. It ruined mine. I sat in her hollow bedroom crying and crocheting a purple chain of yarn with a broken heart.

At the time and every time it was talked about, my parents stated they sent her away because they didn't want her associating with the Native Americans. (Racism was common and openly expressed in those days. Political correctness didn't exist.) I knew that it was because the physical and emotional violence had gotten so bad my parents decided they had to do something…without really facing the problem. It was so much easier than admitting our family was rocked with violence. It would have forced my parents to deal more honestly with their relationship and destabilized the awful homeostasis of our lives.

My sister was expelled from that school after a couple of years for some minor infraction and then chose not to go back. She returned home to do her senior year in high school, but things were never the same for me. She had moved on and our relationship had changed. There was arguing and shouting again. However, not the kind of violence like before she was banished/saved. What I remember is that the conflict between my parents climaxed with my mother threatening to move back to the city whether my father decided to move with her or not. She let him know his presence was not necessary. So, we all moved.

My dad rented a big truck and we drove three hours to the green stucco house on the corner of our street. #2 married her boyfriend and moved to a hovel in rural nowhere. This began a foreign life for me.

In the fifth grade, I was tyrannized by Bob. He was emperor of the popular clique. Little did I realize this was the beginning of a lifelong pattern. I was secretly attracted to the thug, but I was terrified of him ridiculing me in front of everyone. I crept around the elementary school embarrassed that I was a yokel who didn't know enough to brush her teeth. I wore hand me down clothes from strangers, including a poodle skirt with a coffee stain on it which Bob spotted and pointed out at the top of his lungs. I dreaded recess and gym was a disaster. I was almost always chosen last for teams. One other girl was also last and sometimes she was chosen after me. She was a darling, very dainty and well liked. I was introverted and socially inept. My hair was god-awful. At the beginning of the year my mom would take me and # 4 to the beauty shop and say, "Cut it short and give it a tight perm." Then I was on my own. Mom hated hair because it was somehow "sexy".

Bob and his boys were merciless. When I wasn't being humiliated publicly, they teased a boy in the class who was pudgy, odd, and considered a fool. I hate to admit it, but I was relieved when I was not the target. It never occurred to me that I could fight back, stand up for myself, report his ass to the principal. It was a lesson that I repeatedly had to learn. Being assertive was not a "good girl" characteristic. In fact, it was against the rules.

Redoing the fifth grade didn't have any real benefit for me, and my self-esteem took a hit. It was a secret. I told no one except for my only friend, swearing her to secrecy. After all, I was smart and I needed her to know that it was my age that got me held back, not my grades. I was a product of my family, after all. School success was mandatory.

In the 7th grade I fell in love. Mark liked me too…until Bob began to rib him about it. He took me on my first date to a New Year's Eve party at a friend's house. I was in heaven, having taken over my own hair style by then and wearing it in a Jackie Kennedy flip. My fancy party dress had sparkles on a tight fit. When we returned to school in January Mark stopped looking at me in math class. He stopped calling. No more dedicating Beatles songs to me on the radio.

I put on at least 30 pounds in the following five months of that school year. That summer, which was just before #1 broke off with my parents, we went to visit her and my beloved nephew who was just one year old. When she came to the door, she announced in her shrill voice, "Sherry, you're fat. I never thought YOU would be fat."

Remember, fat was and is a big issue in my family. Fat and flawed were the same thing. I stopped eating and turned into a frail apparition, lying on my bed, getting up only to weigh and drink water. I ate 200 calories a day most days and could make those morsels of food last for hours by eating tiny bits at a time. Once, my dad ordered me into the kitchen to "eat something" when he noticed I was wasting away. My mom said, "Leave her alone. She's just dieting." And that was that. The thing that got me eating again was that when school started in the fall I knew I had to eat enough to get up and go pull good grades.

I was still very underweight. My bones stuck out all over and I'd stopped menstruating. I don't remember much about the next two years because I was starving my body and my brain. I got the grades, got braces for my teeth, went home every day from school and put on my head gear (the appliance that helped to straighten my teeth) like a good and responsible girl, did homework, and I hid. In some ways, the focus on academic achievement and my role in the family saved my life. I started eating again.

Throughout my high school years, I cycled through boyfriends. None of them were good at school, which was my area to shine. They also had other, shall we say, less desirable qualities. The guy I started going with after my 7th grade love was someone I met at a swimming pool. He was three years older than I was. He was cute and he loved me. We were into sex but always just barely avoided intercourse, not because I cherished my virginity, but because I was terrified of becoming pregnant. I aspired for college and a career. After Christmas, I broke it up.

I had another boyfriend from school, my own age this time. His less desirable quality was that he was gay. He didn't know it, or maybe he did. We messed around sexually a bit but no more than that. He was never into it as much as I was, and he was swishy. But he was there. I felt had to have a boyfriend and even though I wanted to break up a lot of the time, I was afraid to be without one. We dated for a little over a year and started high school together. His mother forced the breakup due to the absurd rumor started by a friend of mine (or so I thought of her at the time) that I was pregnant. His mom heard the rumor and made it very difficult for us to be together.

About a month after breaking up with a guy, I was happy. I became satisfied being on my own and enjoyed it. Yet for some reason I was always on the lookout for a relationship. I had abandonment issues that were rooted in #2 being sent away from me and the continual conflict between my parents.

I drifted for a while, dated a few boys before finding my final boyfriend and the man who I would marry. He was beautiful, sweet, charming, and artistic. We engaged in sex like we were in heat. This is important to mention, as it was one of the cornerstones of my core belief that I was a good girl. At one point, I thought I was pregnant. We were terrified. I was sick to my stomach with anxiety, which only added to my suspicions of pregnancy. I was in the 11th grade, and he was in the 12th, hardly old enough to be having children. Then, by the grace of the Goddess and pure luck, I started my period. My mother had been observing me and the drama that we were trying to conceal. She asked me if I was sexually active. I confessed, and the next morning she brought in a white pill. We were free to copulate like crazy.

And we did. We did it in cars, in the park at night, in the night shadows at the school near my home, at the church, in the mountains on back roads, at his house and mine when no one was home, everywhere we could. We got caught by police three times in his car. I got sassy once and when the cop asked if my mother knew what I was doing, I said, "Yes. Why don't you call her?" He saw that I was not intimidated and suggested we find someplace else to do the deed. I demanded to know where that would be. That didn't stop us. I simply had to have sex.

I went to college in another city to be near my boyfriend. I didn't want to go to school there. I had different aspirations, but he was there, and I couldn't imagine being without him. I chose the Licensed Practical Nursing Program with the idea that I would graduate after a year then work to support us while he went to school in art. (He really was and still is a brilliant artist.) But he didn't like school, with the exception of the art classes. I hated nursing. At one point, I called my mom and told her I wanted to break up with my boyfriend, go home, and change schools so I could major in something I loved. She said, "Do it. I KNOW YOU WON'T BE PROMISCUOUS."

And there it was. Good girls don't have sex outside marriage, and she had made an allowance for me because I was a good girl, and I was in a monogamous relationship planning to get married. Almost as good. Problem was, I didn't know I wouldn't be promiscuous, and I knew I wanted to be sexual. So, I stayed.

Then my boyfriend enlisted in the Navy with one of his friends, even though he had just given me an engagement ring. The draft for the Viet Nam war began and the lottery gave him #14. Going to war was a sure thing. He decided enlisting would at least prevent him from combat.

He had to have his father's permission. Boys had to be 21 to marry without parental approval at that time in my state. Girls only had to be 18. His father deliberated a long time before signing the form. If I'd had to have parental permission, I have no doubt that my parents would have signed the form post haste. I would then be a legally good girl and in my religious culture getting married young was the norm, not the anomaly.

We didn't want to rock the boat, not ours, not our parents', although I think now that his parents would have been jubilant if we had broken up since we were so young. We were 19.

We got married a couple of months later just before he left for boot camp. I became a nurse. My last name changed, and I began to lose myself. You might think a name change is no big deal. But it disoriented me and made me wonder who I was. I've read about love of another adult, but I don't think I really knew what it was. I always felt intense desire and lust which was nearly eradicated the minute I was married. I mentioned before that I was absolutely addicted to sex with my first husband. It was what I lived for…until we got married.

The night of our wedding we returned to our slum of an apartment, and he just wanted to go to sleep. It was late and we both had school and work the next day. I wanted crazy sex, the kind we had had for the previous two and a half years. Now I can't say if sex had changed for him. But we did have sex and it was different. I didn't experience the transformational state of consciousness I had always experienced during our previous sexual encounters where I felt like I was being compelled out of the top of my head and spinning out into the cosmos. Dramatic picture, I know. Sex was a spiritual, exalted experience for me. Then my wedding night, nothing. What had happened?

I've read about love of another adult; I don't think I knew what it was. I always felt intense desire and lust which was nearly eradicated the minute I was married. I mentioned before that I was absolutely addicted to sex with my first husband. It was what I lived for…until we got married. This began a pattern in my life where I would change my last name based upon my marital status at any given time, along with my identity.

DISCOVERING THE GREAT I AM

We moved to San Diego, California where he was stationed. It was daring, exciting, and I was so homesick that first year. I had to send my little dog back home by airplane to my mom to keep when we couldn't find an apartment that would allow me to keep her. My heart broke. I loved Spanky like a baby. I even had a dream that I gave birth to Spanky and that she died. In the dream I heard myself say, "How can you even think of being a parent to a child if you can't keep a dog alive." I had become pregnant with my first baby and was 20 years old.

Our relationship had been punctuated with conflict from the beginning. I was...wait for it...responsible. So, throughout the relationship I managed and saved the money, paid the bills, worked consistently, and was responsible. He was eccentric and had an achingly free spirit that didn't really have room for a wife and child, even though I believe he loved us. We argued. We were kids with a baby on the way. He ended up being honorably discharged from the navy due to an injury and we decided to return to our home state where he would go to school, and I would work as a nurse to support us; we would have the emotional support of our parents. The plan as I understood it was that after he graduated, he would support me while I went to school. It didn't happen that way. We both had unrealistic expectations.

My husband found it too difficult manage work and school, so he quit work. When the art classes ran out, he stopped going to school. I scheduled us with a marriage counselor.

I was resentful. Sex had become an obligation. The first and only time we met with the counselor I raged about how I felt like I was doing all the work. And he had the audacity to expect me to spread my legs for him too? My husband complained that he wasn't getting enough sex. The counselor sent us out with bad copies of sex exercises. I threw them in the trash on the way out the door.

We split up for one month, got back together, then he decided to hitchhike to California with a friend rather than start the fall semester at school. While he was gone I moved out.

I had established an emotional love relationship with a guy I worked with at the hospital. He was, as he defined himself, "a walk on the wild side" for me. He had a "fuck you" attitude toward the world. I was enamored with his act because I was a coward. Fear dominated me. We could have had an affair. But I was a good girl and still married. I simply ignored that we were having an emotional affair. It wasn't sex so it didn't count.

After I left my first husband the door was "open" and my work buddy lunged through. I was terrified of being on my own, and a feeling of emptiness just simply drove me to jump into a relationship again. And nothing, but nothing had prepared me for this one. It was to be the meat of my journey for the next three decades.

To summarize:

- Being without partner feels like abandonment.
- Assertion is unacceptable in a good girl. Obedience to the rules is expected.
- My goals are secondary to everything else.

Core Belief: I am a good girl.

Chapter 3

EARLY ADULTHOOD

THE LONG LESSON
EPIPHANIES AND OTHER MIRACLES

Although my husband and I had had some good sexual experiences after that, especially when we lived in San Diego before I became pregnant, I never really felt the quality of ecstasy that I had experienced prior to being married. And it went downhill from there. After I had my baby my sex drive vanished. I was overwhelmed, sleep deprived, profoundly disappointed. I didn't realize his goals and needs were not being met either.

Marriage is a flawed system akin to legalized prostitution. A woman changes her name and who she is when she marries. She becomes a possession of her husband. At least that is how it was for me and it has always taken the thrill of sexual individuality and personal choice away. It's that good girl/bad girl thing again. If I'm married, I am a good girl, and if I'm a good girl I don't enjoy sex. Sex became an obligation. It's the belief structure erected in my childhood and has been one of the foundations for my life experience.

It wasn't all my parent's influence. In a patriarchal society, women are valued for their functions of sex and childbearing. We become objects to be owned and controlled. Other women may feel completely different about this; I acknowledge this is just my own story, although I have heard many other women voice the same kind of feelings. But unless one has children, I don't see the point of including the government in one's relationship. Unfortunately, I don't have a better idea for raising children that is at this point in our culture a better alternative.

Five years to the day after we married, my divorce was finalized and in came the man I worked with to be my second husband and fill the vacuum. I didn't even have a chance to process the fact that my marriage was ending before he was well established as the new partner in my life.

With the birth of each of my children, I was madly in love. It is through relationships that we learn and grow, maybe especially from the ones that are the most difficult and the most painful.

Now, I'd be lying if I stated that I was snowballed, although I have told my story that way. Before we got married, I had a gut twisting feeling of self-betrayal screaming at me to end the relationship. But I didn't. Even then the relationship was punctuated with conflict. Fear of the unknown, fear of being on my own (although I had shown myself I could support myself and my baby), fear of sexual promiscuity (there it is again), fear of failure, fear of feeling abandoned, fear, fear, fear.

Over the next few years, I spent a lot of time at work trying to manage our chaotic relationship over the phone, something that my peers at work commented on many times. Of course, this was driven by my own core beliefs about my role. I must again add, this is MY story. I'm sure his is different and I'm not trying to place blame. We were both operating in our own dysfunction. I was a deer in the headlights. My learned response was no response. I felt like a victim.

As a mental health therapist, I have learned since that this dynamic is very common. Simply, it is a system where the individuals feel they need rescuing from their abandonment and the accompanying feelings. If they feel victimized, they behave like a victim, even in the face of facts that may not support this thesis. No amount of evidence could stop the pattern we were in. I was shutting down. I'm sure he saw this as "proof" that I didn't love him which was probably reinforcing to his core belief of being unlovable. For me, it was self-protective.

The healthiest thing to do would have been to end the relationship. I wasn't that healthy. So, I did the next best thing. I went on with my life and built it separate from his. We lived parallel lives. In so many ways I felt like a single parent.

As I stated earlier, I was the good girl who tried to keep the peace and please everyone. Jolting the relationship with the continual thoughts I had of leaving him simply wasn't an option for me. I was too insecure and scared. I was afraid of him as much as I was afraid of being alone. So, I didn't tell him the truth about my feelings. That was assertion beyond my comprehension.

I was passive and had no idea that I could and should assert myself. I really felt that I had no right to declare how I would live my life. How bizarre is that? I did what was familiar. I was "obedient". Ever the good girl.

We were both empty wells expecting the other to fill our emptiness.

The morning after a marriage ceremony at city hall I stood in the linen room at the hospital where I worked, and I cried. I had legally cemented the relationship. My last name changed again. I didn't know who I was or where my childhood self had gone.

I repeated my story over the years to myself and others, becoming more and more resentful. Still, I stayed. Until much later I didn't see my own participation in my oppression and abuse. I felt like a prisoner of war.

After about three years of marriage, we bought our first house. We lived there four months before I left for the first time after a nasty scene in front of my four-year-old daughter as I was trying to leave.

A few days later I took my daughter to my parents for safe keeping and left. I must confess that I had already found a man to fill my emptiness. He and I had flirted, but again I was being good and didn't have a sexual relationship with him until I had left my husband. That "relationship" was over almost as soon as it had been consummated.

I had a drive to go it alone without a man. But when I found myself confronting that empty place inside me, my anxiety skyrocketed.

Years later I ran into the other guy when he was a patient in the hospital where I was working, and he gave me one of the best compliments I've ever had. He looked at me and said, "There were so many girls that I don't remember any of them. But I remember you. You taught me how to think." The other compliment I received like that was from another man I had worked with just prior to that who said I had a "fine mind". Those comments meant a lot to me because, remember, being intelligent was of paramount importance in my upbringing. Apart from being called smart, I was being told I was a thinker. Another friend also suggested I stop talking about my distress and maybe that would motivate me to do something with my situation. That was one of the small awakenings I had early on when I began to realize I had a part to play what I defined as my imprisonment.

During that brief split from my husband, I also dated a bit. I had met someone else at work and went out with him once. He attempted to get me into bed that night and I thought I was ready to be sexual with him. But the minute he made his move I recoiled and apologized saying I couldn't do it. He made another attempt, and I again set the limit. He was a good sport. After all, I had led him on. But that was that. Mom was right. I couldn't be promiscuous. I also knew that I had it in me to be assertive if I decided to be. That's is a lesson I had to learn dozens of times before I even dared to speak my truth.

I came to a startling realization. It was one of the few times in my life I had an awakening that changed the course of my life. I knew with a deep certainty that if I didn't learn the lesson I had set myself up to learn in the relationship with my husband, I would inevitably choose another even more difficult situation in order to learn what I needed to know. I had gone from one husband to another without changing anything about myself. I knew I had to change but had barely an inkling about what to do differently.

This began the process of me learning to disrupt some of my old beliefs. I noticed the constant dialogue running through my head. We all have it. Gurus and mystics have spoken volumes on attempts to silence it. I still didn't understand how I was literally creating my own reality with my thoughts, but knew that I had to put a stop to the constant chatter in my head arguing with myself about whether or not to leave the marriage. Changing one's thinking isn't as easy as it sounds. I became vigilant at focusing my thoughts and I made a conscious decision to stay and to stop the internal battling.

I was reading a lot of Castaneda's stuff and other books as well looking for answers and understanding only a tiny bit of what was written. Don Juan Matis in Carlos Castaneda's books called it "stopping the world". He was referring to stopping the judging and criticism and all the internal dialogue holding the story in place, my story of helplessness.

I was 27 when we got back together after that split and things again began to fall back into old patterns. There was an incident between us, one of hundreds. But I opened my mouth and refused to behave compliantly. Assertiveness at last! Unfortunately, my conviction to speak up wavered a lot over most of the rest of the relationship for years, ebbing and flowing like something unanchored. I developed an overwhelming need to reconnect with my spirituality.

I had been living as an atheist since about the age of 16. And suddenly, there it was. A giant hole inside me needing that connection with spirit that I had experienced as a little child. I remembered that feeling of "talking" with spirit, not the rote prayers I had said with my mom as we knelt by my bed at night, but the real talking I had done with whatever that is that resides deep within everything. I began searching for my lost self.

When I was 16, I had distanced myself from our family religion in tandem with my mother who was also going through her own exit. We were both reading the existential writers. Whenever I would ask questions in church meetings about doctrine, I would hear the rationale that Satan was able to overtake my thinking when I allowed myself to question, so I should never question. Then too, having sex outside marriage was creating extreme cognitive dissonance for me. I felt hypocritical going to church, being involved in discussion in my young women's group about the evils of premarital sex while waiting for the next opportunity to engage in it. I was leading two lives, the good religious girl expected to save her chastity for marriage and the bad girl loving sex outside marriage. Mom had put me on the pill; so, I was safe. Agnosticism and atheism made sense to me.

As I stated in the beginning of this book, Mom saw that I was being sexual and ended up going to two different doctors to get a prescription for birth control, one for herself and one for me. It was illegal, or at least unheard of, to prescribe the pill to an unmarried woman, especially a teen. Condoms couldn't even be purchased by someone underaged. I will always love her for this. In those days when a girl became pregnant, she was often sent to live in a home for unwed mothers, her baby was adopted out, and she was marked for life. She was expelled from school, but the father of the baby was not. At that time, there were no alternative or night schools, no GED. The girl often became a social outcast until, if she were lucky enough, some guy married her to make her respectable again. I knew of only one girl who managed to return to high school after her baby was born, with special permission from the school district and the insistence of her influential family. She had also married the father of her baby.

I only knew two ways of spiritual being-ness. Like my mother I was either involved in our religion or atheist. My young daughter and I were out walking one day, and she asked me if I believed in God. I told her I didn't and that I didn't feel like I needed a God in my life. She told me that she did believe, and that "God talks to me". I was surprised as I had never exposed her to the idea of a God and didn't know where she would have gotten that notion. I felt like I had permission to reembrace that lost part of myself. After all, as a child I had talked with God, or whatever that is.

I headed back to church. It met my need. But I was always at odds with the doctrine. I began to pay tithing to the church out of my paycheck, as this was basic to inclusion in my church. That caused quite a row with my husband. Somehow, I found the strength to assert myself and paid it anyway. I remember musing that, although it remained a source of conflict between us, I had set a limit and I felt stronger.

I kept the fact that my spiritual experiences were outside the norm of the religion a secret for the most part. My best friend commented to me that I wasn't really a believer and continually questioned my identification with the religion. Then something profound happened to me.

I had gone to the dentist for a routine filling where nitrous oxide was just beginning to be used. I was miserable. There was nothing specific that I can remember that might have triggered this experience, just the same old accusations of infidelity, criticisms, and awfulness that had become the script of my life. I must have been looking for some way out.

I distinctly remember a sense of speeding up and dissolving. I became formless. I retained my ego identity, but it felt distant and asleep. I knew everything! There were no questions, only answers. And I felt the love. It wasn't love like I had felt for my family, men, or even my child. It was the fabric of all creation, complete and indescribable. Everything moved to a rhythm or a vibration, but it was much more than that. It was woven into the fabric of existence and inseparable from it. I floated in this endless bath of love and knowledge, and I was aware of nothing else. I was whole, and I was perfect.

I suddenly felt I was being sucked back into my tiny, constricted physical reality. I didn't want to go, but realized I had to. "Please, let me remember something of this," I begged. Then I was back. But I remembered something of what I had known…

I AM GOD, GOD IS EVERYTHING, EVERYTHING IS ME, LIKE THE MOTHER IS THE CHILD, BUT MUCH MORE INTIMATELY. AND THE NATURE OF GOD…ANDROGENY.

That event, more than any, changed my life forever. It was not a metaphor. It was and is reality. I knew any perceived divisions between myself and others or any other part of creation is an illusion. I knew that everything is consciousness, even things that didn't seem to be conscious. I knew that I was both the creator and the created, the dreamer and the dream. It has sustained me in my struggle to evolve spiritually and given me hope and strength when I felt despair. It became my talisman.

I must say here that I have had nitrous oxide at least 20 times over the years since then and none of them have led to a spiritual experience, not even close. I believe that experience was triggered by my profound desperation for escape from my misery. Something inside me saw an exit and I fled. For decades after that my goal was to re-experience that oneness I'd felt when I blended with All Consciousness.

My spiritual drive eventually led me to go back to my childhood town, to my father's school where he had been the principal, to the church I went to as a child with the painting of Jesus Christ in the Garden of Gethsemane over the pulpit, to the house my father built for us, to the red rock hill where I spent days adventuring and dreaming.

I found myself standing at the pulpit in the church where I had stood at age 8, freshly baptized and reciting "How Great the Wisdom and The Love" as the organist played the music in the background. I sat in a pew crying and embracing my childhood self while apologizing to her for dragging her through the mess of my life. I laid on the red rock "down over the hill", as I called it, where I had spent hours as a child and felt myself blend with the heat and the waffling leaves on the quaking aspen tree growing out of the hot dirt. I walked the halls of the condemned elementary school and retraced the distantly familiar pattern of the tiles of the floor in the lavatory where Debbie, Loraine, and I had twirled in front of the huge mirror with our skirts flattening out like pancakes. I brought the child that I was back home into my body and felt those fragments fuse with the frazzled entity I had become. Driving back to the city that night looking out at the stars I had spun through as a child while camping out in my backyard, I felt myself healing. I was becoming whole again.

So, my husband I were off and running down the same path of dysfunction. I became vigilant in my resolve to set my boundaries and limits. I knew that was what I was supposed to learn. But I was a very slow learner. My children have commented often that he and I were always arguing. Yes, we were. It wasn't so much that we argued *all the time*. But the tension was in our energy *all the time*, and yes, we argued too. But I came to really understand his pain and to have empathy for him. Still, my own emotional survival kept me guarded and inhibited. I lived in survival mode.

For every limit I set there were dozens of situations I tolerated. I was afraid I would be abandoned, alone, scared. I was amazed when I did confront him about something the outcome often lifted our relationship an increment higher. I got pregnant again, twice more, which put me into a position of financial dependence. That held me in place, that and my belief that I couldn't survive alone with my children without his financial support. I don't want to debate with myself anymore whether that was true. The material thing here is that it was what I believed. I was living inside of my story and was hypnotized by it.

It was very new for me to be assertive in any way. But each time, I got stronger. I began the long arduous process of learning that my life is my creation, and I am not a victim or bystander. As I've said before, I came to know this intellectually. But I didn't know it on an experiential level, and my insecurities and faulty beliefs were still very much intact.

There are differences in knowing. I have found that the deep knowing that comes with spiritual awakening is, at least for me, long after I have learned something intellectually many times over. My fear of the unknown would be my battleground in so many different scenarios.

I read every book I could on "new age" philosophy, self-help books, the mystical and magical, and eventually quantum physics. My soul needed both intellectual and spiritual understanding, while being grounded in the reality of my imploding life.

My father told me once in the early chaotic days of my marriage when I broke down in front of him that I needed to "toughen up". I loved him so much for saying that, since I had developed the mistaken core belief that I had to be submissive and "go along" or risk not being the good girl I believed I had to be. I'd been given permission to say, "Hell no". I've found in my work with those in similar life situations it's important for them to hear someone say, "You have a right to say no".

I left my church again after realizing that it was simply too confining and rigid, and that it was no longer meeting my spiritual needs. I not only left my church, I left religion as a whole.

My daughters were beginning to show the disturbance that comes when children grow up in a chaotic and unpredictable environment. My oldest daughter was 15. I had hit a plateau. As I rounded the corner near our house on my way to work one day I said to the universe, "OK. I'm ready for the next step." And with that, my next lesson was upon me.

The following day one of my daughter's teacher called to say she had had a meltdown in class and that same afternoon my oldest daughter came to me and told me to find her somewhere else to live. She told me she wanted to go live with her biological father in another city, and that if she couldn't go there, she would find some place.

It was as though I suddenly became possessed with superpowers. I moved from inertia to motion. I found a two-bedroom apartment to rent, found a full-time position in a nursing home (yuck, but worth it if it meant freedom), put my two youngest at my parent's house for the night, arranged for my oldest to spend the night at her friend's house, and prepared to confront my husband with an ultimatum.

I returned home after distributing my kids to see my husband sitting at the kitchen table. He immediately picked up on something being different. Now, here is the weird part. As I opened the front door, I felt the left side of my mind turn and face the right and say, "Be quiet and let me handle this." I realize this sounds bizarre. But it was as tactile and as profound as that.

I presented my ultimatum, convinced that he would never go for it. But he did and we agreed to get help. I had mixed feelings about this. Half of me had wanted him to refuse. My oldest daughter did go live with her father for a year and some things improved between me and my husband. But he was the same man, and I was the same woman. The family dysfunction and individual distresses continued.

Still, I was becoming more assertive. I *was* changing. The spiritual experiences continued.

I had my first aware out of body experience sleeping on the couch in the living room where I slept often. I woke up while walking through the closed front door. The living room had a dull red glow about it and my body was prone on the couch. I felt instant horror. **IT** was coming up the basement stairs and was going to, I don't know, annihilate me.

Instantly, I was hovering above my sleeping body, half in and half out of the top of my head. I tried to swim back into my body, but fear froze me. Then I remembered what Juan Matis had told Carlos when he was having terrifying other-worldly experiences. He had told him to "shift his focus" from one object to another. This would prevent him from getting lost in the fear he was manifesting within that experience. When I did that, my fear dissolved momentarily, then I'd remember it and another bout of terror was ignited. I just kept hovering partly in and partly outside my body for a long time. Eventually, I re-entered my body, woke up and then drifted back to sleep. I continued to catch myself floating up out of the top of my head off and on that night, waking to reorient myself then drifting back to sleep until morning.

I became determined to have more out of body experiences. I'd occasionally take my waking self into dreams, then fall back to sleep. I couldn't control anything. I remember once waking up in a dream and finding myself playing in the branches of the tree that grew by my childhood home, floating and dancing from branch to branch. At one point, I became determined to make an out of body experience happen. I walked into my bedroom in full daylight, lay on my bed fully awake, and willed myself to leave my body. I even had my eyes open. I felt my consciousness rise up in my body almost leaving it, freaked out, and fell solidly back into it on the bed. That was the last time I had a conscious or waking out of body, until recently.

Lucid dreaming has spontaneously occurred for me throughout my life. Once in a particularly frightening dream I was having when I was very young, I simply said to myself, "Don't worry. You can always wake up." It became something that I could do after that. The frightening dreams I had as a child usually involved me running or flying to escape something, which was on my heals grabbing at me. The dreams took place in our church, or my dad's elementary school, or outside our house. Those terrifying dreams repeated themselves until I learned to either wake up or recognize in the dream that they were just dreams, and then leave them.

Little did I realize then that my current "reality" is a dream that a higher entity is having, and that I can wake from it or change it at will just by exiting the dream. (Row, Row, Row Your Boat…)

I hated nursing and found the work disgusting. In those days, nurses were women and doctors were men. It bugged me that nurses were expected to be submissive to the doctors. After several years, I came to believe that I would likely be there for the rest of my life, so I became determined to make the best of it. I stopped resisting and accepted my life, even finding some satisfaction in my work. Then as so often happens, once I learned the lesson in front of me, everything changed. An opportunity to move to another hospital close to home working with my best friend in a great nursing job became mine.

It was during that time that I ran into the guy I'd had the fling with 10 years before when my husband and I were separated. His comment to me that I'd taught him how to think triggered me to go back to school so that I could finally extricate myself from nursing and do something I wanted to do.

I worked 32 hours on the weekends and went to school during the week for my bachelor's degree, then went on to graduate school. I got a master's in clinical social work and then my LCSW. I was finally free of nursing and following something I felt passionate about.

One night when I was particularly discouraged, I had a dream. It was one of those dreams where I was consciously present and aware that I was dreaming. I was in a car with my husband who was driving. There were diamonds which had spilled on the floor, and I was frantically trying to pick them up. There were people outside the car on my right sitting at tables eating and watching us. I was concerned that they would see the diamonds. I was bending over trying to pick them up when suddenly my husband said, "Look! There's God." I sat up and said, "Where?" He replied, "Everywhere."

As I gazed around, I experienced a repeat of the deep knowing that God is everything and everywhere, a brief re-experiencing of the dentist chair experience from nearly 20 years before. I remember looking out of the car seeing the beautiful deep and glowing colors around me, particularly green. Everything was alive with consciousness, and I was part of it. More accurately, everything was me.

I have wondered at the significance of me dreaming that my husband told me that God was everywhere. The man I had a conflicted relationship with had reminded me of my own divinity and his as well. These kinds of experiences have occurred when I am in my highest degree of distress, and my marriage certainly did create that. I don't know if I would have had these experiences which I cherish so much if I had been peacefully happy with my life. I don't think so.

I had begun to read about quantum physics and had become aware of how thoughts and actions can move and influence energy. I had also become very interested in Wicca and spell binding. I had taken workshops, gone on women's spiritual retreats, and always consulted my books on the different and unusual. One day, I was sitting in the living room alone. I visualized a long energetic cord, like an electric cord, running from my third chakra to my husband who was in the bedroom. (The 3rd chakra is where personal power resides and is near the naval.) I sat in the silent and dusky living room visualizing myself grabbing the cord out of my naval and throwing it away from my body. I even used the physical motions of pulling and throwing. Within two seconds he came out of the bedroom and into the living room and asked, "What did you just do?" He had felt something.

Each year on our wedding anniversary I would ask myself, "Are things any better than they were last year?" Some years it was a big "yes". Some years it was a tiny "yes". But it was only the last couple of years of the marriage, after my cancer diagnosis, that I stopped asking. Cancer was taking me in a different direction, whether I wanted to go.

The last time we had sex was right after I was diagnosed with bilateral breast cancer. For the following three years until I left him, I was even more distant. We bought a big new house, which was something he had wanted to do for a while. I went along with it, but even now I'm not sure why. Maybe it was the desire to leave cancer and the rest of the painful stuff behind. Maybe it was the desire to start over. I'd had mastectomies, chemotherapy, and radiation and needed change. Then my youngest daughter got married…and something snapped inside me. I found myself making concrete plans to leave my marriage.

It happened, as if I was not part of the decision. My husband and I drove to the courthouse for her wedding ceremony. I knew I was going to leave him and this time there was no going back. When I told him a few days later what was happening, I could see he was resigned to it. We both knew it had been coming for the entire time we had been together, and I sensed some resignation that it was finally really happening. He said he loved me to which I replied, "Then let me go." He did.

I have heard that it takes half as long as the relationship lasted to get over it completely and move on. I don't know if that is accurate, but it took me about 13 years to fully come to terms with the previous 27 years, to let go of the anger, and to accept responsibility for my decision to live my life the way I had.

For the better part of my marriage, I'd had a repeating dream every few weeks. I dreamed that I had to choose between my first and second husband. I had never been able to process the dissolution of my first marriage and still felt like I needed a relationship. In those dreams, I would choose one and then the other, either way feeling like I'd made a mistake. I would wake up sick at heart. What was the point in them? Why?

Then one night about two years after my second divorce while living on my own I had the dream again. I experienced the anxiety of deciding, the turmoil of knowing that either choice would be a mistake, and the agony of feeling like I was messing up my life. Suddenly, I heard my own voice say, "You don't have to choose either one." And that was the last time I had the dream.

What I learned:

- I am responsible for every bit of my life.
- I can only control my choices.
- If I do not live authentically and true to myself, my body will get sick.
- My spiritual development will take me where I need to go.
- AND THE BIG ONE: **I am God, God is everything, everything is me.** All else is illusion.

Chapter 4

THE GIFT

**You Are Not Your Thoughts. You Are Not Your Feelings.
You are a divine fractal of the God-consciousness
creating a human experience.
—Sherry Griffith, LCSW**

The first winter I lived alone in my 100-year-old home I lay on the basement floor crying because I was afraid of lighting the pilot light on the furnace. What I finally figured out was that there wasn't one. I turned on the thermostat and the furnace kicked on. That's pretty much how I learned to do things by myself. I dug a small fishpond in my back yard with a fountain after successfully breaking down the cement borders and eliminating the field of weeds. I began to remodel my house, from ceiling fans to adding an entire wing on the back of the house. I tore out the grass in front and put in a xeriscape. Planted a tree and bushes. Redid the floors in the older part of the house. Then I painted on the walls; not painted the walls, which I did as well. But I painted giant flowers on them. My house became the manifestation of what was inside me. I was healing.

I found myself pulling away from my children and my best friend. The overwhelming desire for peace of mind meant isolation. I was drained, directionless, and there was that deep need to be alone. Then Abby became sick.

Abby was my oldest daughter's youngest baby. She was about 6 months old when she began to lose weight and get pneumonia. She was diagnosed with failure to thrive. But why? Her father suspected something was wrong with her immune system. He was right. She was nearly dead when the diagnosis was confirmed. She had Severe Combined Immune Deficiency Syndrome, SCIDS. She needed a bone marrow transplant. Even with a transplant the life expectancy reached only young adulthood. My family went into grief. And for the next four years Abby's life was fragile.

My daughter found a psychic to come to the hospital. The woman, whom we had never met but had been recommended by a friend, met with us and looked at Abby lying in her hospital crib. We were in a small room off Hobbi's room behind a window with the light out watching her as we talked. The psychic stated that Abby had communicated to her that she didn't know if she wanted to stay in this life, she was undecided, and that Abby had chosen this incarnation to be part of something bigger. I remember Abby, unable to see anything but our shadows at the most, looked at the window the entire time. She was intubated and had a pic line delivering medication and nutrition into her blood stream. Her prognosis was grim.

Abby ended up having a stem cell transplant. It was disastrous and for the next two years she was on the verge of death due to graft versus hosts disease (her body rejecting the transplant) and to the treatment that kept her alive. She was swollen and miserable. My daughter told Abby that she wanted her to stay so that she could see who she was without being sick. Abby managed to stay alive but was so close to death when her parents demanded a new transplant that it was not certain she would make it through the process of total body radiation and chemotherapy. There really was no other choice. The graft versus host disease from the stem cells was killing her.

After some months of looking for an appropriate donor, one was found in Germany. A woman in her 50's. This transplant worked and Abby began to thrive, started dance classes, tumbling, and kindergarten. Then in the second month of kindergarten, Abby fell and knocked out a tooth. This resulted in meningitis, and she died the next day after running high fevers. But that night she said something profound.

She was talking to her dad and said something to him about butterflies watching her. When she died the next day in the same PICU room that she had been in when diagnosed five years earlier, the entire extended family and her grandparents were there. We were in our own spaces of grief when we noticed the ceiling of the room and the door frames were covered with decorative butterflies. We had her memorial at the Make a Wish Foundation. Abby had been a poster child for them and had toured schools and facilities to educate people about the foundation. At her memorial, we released wild butterflies outside into the garden in her honor.

Grief is quite the teacher. I felt grief for my daughter, her husband, their older daughter who was herself just a small child. I felt grief for Abby. I felt grief for my other children and grandchildren, and for myself. I can now see that Abby didn't ever intend to live this life for very long. She finished her work then she left. Her staying as long as she did was a gift for her parents and sister. But when she was old enough for the world to begin eclipsing the memory of who she really was, she chose to leave.

I believe that was Hobbi's last incarnation and that she has moved on to other realities. Abby would have been a young adult now had she lived. Yet the events of the day of her death are clear in my memory and it feels like it just happened. She has visited her aunt, me, and her mother since her death. Of course, none of that stops the pain of missing her. But she is there. The entity that gave rise to her personality is there. And she is still part of our lives.

I have watched my other grandchildren grow and become interesting people with different personalities and gifts. I marvel at what good parents my daughters are, and two of them have terrific husbands whom I love. In spite of their childhoods and setbacks, my daughters are doing well. I am so proud of them and of my grandchildren who continue to amaze me with their unique personalities and achievements.

Abby suffered so much in her tiny body for nearly her entire life. And she did it without complaint. Her poor sister only had one parent at a time while Abby was hospitalized that first four years. When her mom was home her father was in the hospital with Abby, and vice versa. The pain never goes away, I've learned. It's just that you get to where you don't live in the middle of it all the time. When Finding Nemo pictures suddenly appear in my world or the music from Brother Bear or Ice Age comes in an advertisement on TV, I still feel the intense emotion that I felt when she was alive and I watched those movies with her in the hospital. She loved them. I cherish the memories I have of holding her while we watched them on her bed or in the rocking chair. She knew all the dialogue.

Death. We expect grief to be a linear process and a rather fast one. It is neither. It is all consuming for quite some time. Then as life begins to filter back in, it ebbs and flows unpredictably. What is certain is that it is never finished. It is gradually assimilated into the fabric of our lives and becomes part of our stories. We integrate it to the extent that we understand it, to the extent that we can find meaning in our suffering. It forces our stories open and revises our basic beliefs and ideas. It changes our reality for the better, although it is extremely painful.

Grief enlarges our perspective and forces us to feel what we want to avoid feeling, to incorporate new understandings of ourselves and of reality. For many of us, it is the catalyst to begin a new spiritual journey. At the very least, it either reaffirms our beliefs or challenges them.

I have never found it hard to believe in things that are neither provable nor acceptable to society. I attribute that to my upbringing in my childhood religion. All religions have dogma and stories attached to them. The creation stories of most religions and cultures are at the very least bizarre and extraordinary. And my ex-religion is replete with the bizarre and extraordinary. Having come from that background, where it was preached that the one and only true God speaks in person to the prophet of the church, prepared me to accept things that many people raised in more traditional systems couldn't accept. I am prepared to give any idea the benefit of the doubt. I don't believe everything, but I accept that anyone can believe anything, and that belief is the biggest part of what forms individual reality.

As a psychotherapist and a teacher to graduate students, I learned a great deal about cognitive behavioral therapy. As the theory goes, we form our own realities from our core beliefs. From the time we are born we are schooled to believe in a specific reality. As we grow up, the messages we receive about who we are, the nature of the world and our place in it form those core beliefs. We are reinforced when our beliefs and behaviors and emotions match with the environmental forces that formed them. Basic behaviorism shows us that behaviors which are attended to are reinforced by virtue of that attention, and those that are ignored or not given attention tend to disappear. Even painful reinforcement will perpetuate a behavior. I suggest that this goes even further.

There is no one "reality", at least not that we as human beings can know in our ordinary awareness. Rather, there is a field of energy and formation of that energy. We literally create our reality, in conjunction with everyone else, based upon our beliefs about it. We grow up believing that if we have experiences outside the norm about what is real, they are just imagination, a result of mental illness or, worst case scenario, they are evil.

I recently visited Denver. As I sat in the plaza surrounded by enormous multistoried buildings and listening to the music of a live band, I had a perceptual experience.

I looked up at the buildings towering into the sky. I experienced that they were created by me and those in the plaza with me by our subliminal agreement with each other and with the energy surrounding us. We, based upon our conditioning and beliefs, were continually constructing the buildings...literally through our thoughts and the emotions generated by them. And when I turned away from the scene, I stopped using my attention, focus, and will to create them. I knew they continued to exist for others who were still focusing on them, but for me they didn't exist. I was no longer participating in them becoming physical. Or, as I should say, I no longer participated in organizing the energy and then perceiving it with my neurological system, which gives shape and meaning to the organization of that energy. The alternate scene I was focusing on didn't exist when I turned my attention back toward the buildings. Only the scene in front of me was real and existed because that is where my focus was and where I was part of organizing the energy.

This is borne out by discoveries in quantum physics.

Most people have heard the philosophical question: "If a tree falls in the forest and no one is there, does it make a sound?" The implication is that the energy forming the forest scene exists, although the form it takes is in question since the very act of observation automatically organizes it into what our preconceived expectations and beliefs tell us it is. But the sound waves created by the falling tree are "soundless" because hearing sound is about perception. Without the neurological system of a receiver of those waves, there is just the wave…no sound. More to the point, if none of the senses perceive the trees, there are no trees.

The buildings I observed in Denver had a quality of being loosely formed, for a better explanation. I was keenly aware that energy was buzzing around everywhere and that some of it was coagulated into those structures, directed by my expectation and by others to do so. The buildings were our agreed upon construction. This is an unconscious process; one we are all involved in all the time.

I know from quantum physics that this is how reality works for all of us. Quantum physics is both provable sometimes and at other times only theoretical. It deviates from Newtonian physics in that it breaks physical "laws" previously believed to be firm. Einstein referred to the behavior of quanta, or subatomic particles, as "spooky action at a distance". He was referring to how particles will move in conjunction with each other instantaneously even when they are separated by massive distances, as though they were hooked to each other in some way. They are.

In the "Double Slit Experiment", photons (particles of light) were shot through slits in cardboard and followed to a screen on the other side. When the photons were observed, it was discovered that the expectations of the observers influenced where the photons hit on the screen and whether they behaved as a particle (when focused upon) or as a wave when observation was indirect.

Then there are the experiments of Masaru Emoto. He did many experiments with water in which he exposed water to diverse types of music while it was being frozen. The water that was exposed to classical music formed beautiful crystals, even when it started out badly polluted. When exposed to acid rock, the crystals were distorted. It turns out that the type of music was not what was instrumental (pun?). It was the expectations of the observers who were also hearing the music that determined the outcome of crystal formation.

Dr. Emoto also experimented with rice. He placed a bowl of cooked rice in a classroom of his university students with a note that said something like, "Tell the rice it's ugly and you hate it". Then on another bowl of cooked rice he put a note saying, "Tell the rice it is beautiful, and you love it". He found that the hated rice spoiled quickly, and the loved rice stayed good up to 10 times longer. These experiments have been replicated over and over with the same kind of results, proving that the intention of the observer has everything to do with the development of the outcome of the water crystals and the rice. These and other experiments demonstrate that on a massive scale we are all forming reality, individually and collectively. And all without conscious awareness. (Emoto, 2010.)

What if we could become conscious of this process? What could we create? And what are we creating in mass right now, unconsciously? Is it the world we want?

Quantum physics shows us that everything is energy. The entire universe, including people, are just pure energy. Very simply put, everything is made up of minute particles, and when these quanta are not observed, they behave like a wave. The act of observation/expectation "freezes" them into particles of energy/ matter which are then organized by our thoughts, emotions, and into "material" objects, such as water, air, trees, stones, our bodies, etc. Therefore, our thoughts and emotions literally create the world we live in.

As humans, we have long believed that the outer world is more real than our inner world. But the truth is that the inner world IS reality which is projected outward as a hologram into the physical world. Our neurological systems perceive that projection, and our brain interprets its meaning based upon our core beliefs. This leads to a feedback process where the meaning and the hologram influence each other to form individual and collective reality. This is so very important to understand, as humanity is facing cataclysmic events such as perpetual war, climate change, depleted resources, and the collapse of social institutions all over the world. If humanity is to succeed in mitigating the effects of this destruction and rebuild something better, we will need to realize that it all starts on an individual level realizing that we create everything and we can consciously select other alternatives to our present stories.

Back to cognitive behavioral theory. The theory states that we develop a central or core set of beliefs about ourselves and the world. These beliefs are based upon what we are taught by those around us and reinforced through validation of one kind or another. Some people believe they are flawed and worthless, while others believe they are powerful and worthwhile. Some will believe they are helpless and victimized by others, while some will believe they are in charge of their experiences and can make a difference. These core beliefs are influenced by our disposition, our social learning based upon the reinforcement and influence of others, by feedback from our environment, and based upon how we attribute meaning to our experiences. As a wise man once said, "If we think we are a failure, we are". Likewise, if we believe we are anything, we are.

Taken a step further, there is no wrong or right, no good or bad, no black or white in the eternal scheme of things. Rather, we give meaning to the neutral series of events and data from our environment based upon our preconceived ideas about reality, about ourselves, our world, and others in the world. If we believe the world is not a safe place, we will likely behave in such a way as to protect ourselves from perceived danger, expect ourselves to be vulnerable to harm, and to see danger everywhere. Our focus will be in that direction based upon our belief that the world is dangerous, and we are vulnerable to it. We may carry a gun or other weapon, take self-defense classes, install alarms in our homes, have multiple locks on our doors, take out insurance in the event that we have a catastrophe happen. We all seem to do some of this stuff. But when we step back, if we can keep a clear and objective mind, I believe we will see that the real evidence shows that people who do the big protective things are no more "safe" than those who don't. And, in fact, those people who believe that the world is dangerous will end up experiencing it as just that, while another person with similar world experiences will not if they have a more positive view of world.

I had a good friend who helped me open my mind when I was in my early 20's. He said to me, "safety is an illusion." At the time, I wasn't sure what he meant. But it now makes sense. If one looks at the Law of Attraction it states that we will manifest whatever we focus on, which is directed by our beliefs. If we focus on how we are victimized, guess what. We will be. If we focus on health, we will be healthy. If we focus on happiness, we will be happy. It makes sense. We attract what we attend to, what we focus on. This applies on a physical level as well as a spiritual or paranormal one. Manifestation may take a while because we are operating in a medium of very sluggish, slow energy. Four-dimensional reality vibrates at a low frequency. But what we focus our attention on will manifest.

The theory also states that our ideas and thoughts are based upon our core beliefs, which lead to our emotions, thoughts, and behaviors. Those things reinforce each other, with the effect of strengthening our core beliefs. That is how our brain forms our reality. If our core beliefs are maladaptive and leading to our unhappiness, that is detrimental to us. And that is where our core beliefs must be challenged, leading to life changes. As flawed human beings, we dismiss any information that doesn't fit with our already established core beliefs about ourselves and the world. We only assimilate data which we can fit neatly into our already established paradigms of belief. Data that doesn't fit is either invalidated or we literally forget about it. However, if we are functioning consciously, with the goal of changing our experience, the routinely rejected data can be used to challenge our faulty beliefs and to change them to beliefs which form a reality more to our liking. It's called cognitive restructuring in therapist speak, and it is very effective.

When I am doing therapy with a client, I usually start with a psychoanalytic approach, what happened and what effect it had on the individual, their STORY as they believe it to be. This is the beginning of the individual exposing their core beliefs. But then real therapy begins to happen. I work with the client to identify data that either supports their (helpful) beliefs or that will challenge their (destructive) beliefs. We work to challenge beliefs that are limiting and keep the individual from fully functioning and being a "whole" individual. That is how change is made. It is the core of Magic.

To explain this, a diagram may be helpful. All thoughts, emotions, and behaviors are generated by the core belief. In a closed system, such as the cognitive loop, no new information gets in and no protected information gets out. The core belief goes unchallenged, unnoticed even, and doesn't change. That's the reason most of us tend to have the same life lesson over and over. As long as the core belief is untouched, we will manifest what we historically always have. The ego is adept at keeping the system closed. It selectively chooses the external data that it incorporates.

If my core belief is that I am stupid, my thoughts will tell me that over and over, I will behave in a manner consistent with this belief, and I will select the feedback from the environment that validates that belief. My thoughts, emotions, and behaviors will reinforce each other, and they will all reinforce the core belief. The belief is so basic to our self-formed reality that it is never questioned, never challenged, and is regarded as absolute truth. This process holds true regardless of the nature of the core belief or how it gets formed.

The Cognitive Loop

> All information is neutral. We give it meaning based upon our core beliefs about ourselves and the world.

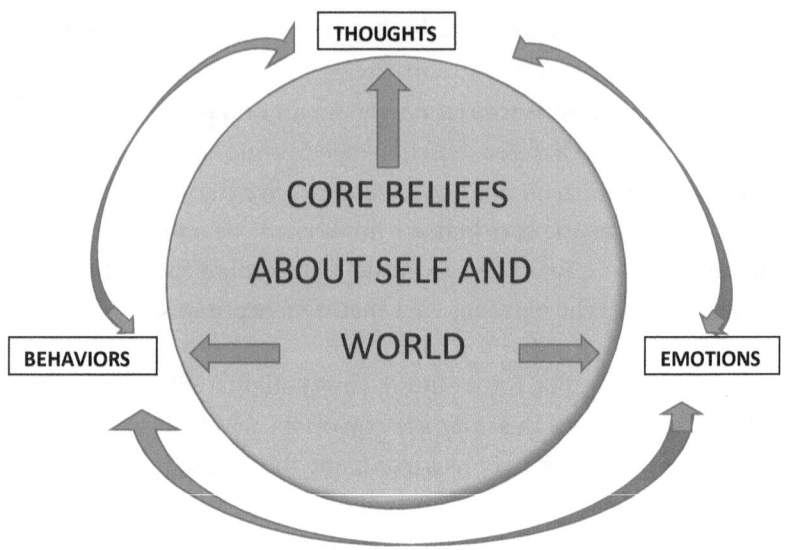

Functional cognitive loop systems are open and allow information out and new information in.

> Functional systems are flexible, adapt to new information, and change to support the individual.
> In order to change our lives we must become functional.
> We then allow this new information to change our core beliefs and therefore, our lives change.
> People who are functional can operate in the gray area and allow for a full range of feelings.

Dysfunctional cognitive loop systems are closed are and rigid. They don't allow any new information in or information out.

- All information taken in is either fit into core beliefs or is rejected rather than allowed to reform the core beliefs.
- Dysfunctional people think in rigid black and white terms of right and wrong, of good and bad.
- Uncomfortable emotions are not tolerated

Often in my practice I see people who are stuck in the past, who are caught up in believing their story. They want to tell and retell the perceived injustices others have perpetrated upon them. They want to blame others for how they feel, behave, and the choices they have made for themselves. After a brief telling of their story so that I can begin to drill down to their destructive core belief, we begin the cognitive restructuring process.

For example, I have known clients who have maintained that a belief they hold is correct, and the evidence they will give for this is "my father told me so", or "that is what I was taught", or "that is just the way things are". They will hold steadfastly to their beliefs and reject evidence to the contrary unless they want to change. Take Marie (I'll call her). She was convinced that everyone victimized her. Our session went something like this:

Marie: Everyone abuses me and I'm not going to let it happen anymore. That clerk saw me and deliberately ignored me. (Marie was ordered by the court to see a therapist to help her manage her anger after she attacked a customer service agent in a store for "ignoring" her.)

Me: Who abuses you?

Marie: Everyone. Everyone!

Me: Was my secretary abusive to you?

Marie: Well, no. But that's just because she is a nice person.

Me: Am I abusive with you?

Marie: Not yet. But I expect you will eventually abuse me too. Everyone does.

Me: So you are presuming that I will abuse you at some point?

Marie: I'm sure you will. Everyone does. I can tell by the look on your face you don't like me. You're probably thinking about what you can do to hurt me. Maybe you'll block me from getting off probation because you don't like me.

Me: Wow. You have already decided that I am going to hurt you and you have even determined how I will do that, all in 30 seconds of our meeting. What evidence do you have that I will abuse you?

Marie: The look on your face. It's like the look the clerk had and everyone gets with me, like they can't stand me.

Me: Tell me about how the look on my face tells you all that.

Marie: Well, you aren't smiling.

Me: So, if I am not smiling that means I don't like you?

Marie: Yeah

Me: Wow. So, if you don't smile at people, does that mean you don't like them and will be abusive with them? Where did you ever get the idea that everyone must be smiling at you, or they don't like you?

Marie: I don't know. My mom used to sneer at me.

Me: So, your mom sneered at you, and she didn't like you? And if everyone doesn't smile it means they don't like you? What other reason might I have for not smiling at you?

Marie: I don't know. You are tired and you don't want to have to see me?

Me: I could be tired. I could be in pain with my arthritis. I could be hungry. Maybe my relaxed face isn't one with a smile. Most people don't smile all the time. Some of us when we get older have "bitch face" when we are relaxed. If I smile at you while we are discussing your issues, would you assume I was laughing at you, making fun of you?

Marie: I don't know. People do that to me too.

Me: Is it possible that people may have an expression on their faces without it having anything to do with you at all, such as if they are hungry, in pain, angry with themselves or their bosses, tired, or just have a face that droops into their expression when they are at rest and listening to you?

(Long Pause.)

Marie: Maybe. But why do they treat me bad then?

Me: How did the clerk treat you badly?

Marie: She ignored me.

Me: Is it possible she didn't see you, or that she was preoccupied with something else, like a problem with another customer or someone else? Is it possible she was experiencing something disturbing to her and she just didn't notice you?

Marie: I guess. But isn't it her job to help me?

Me: So, when you approach someone and assume they are going to abuse you, how do you think your face looks? What might it be conveying to them?

Marie: I don't know. (Pause.) I guess I would be looking at them and frowning.

Me: And is it possible that when the clerk or someone else sees you looking at them and frowning it may make them think you are angry with them, or at least discontented.

Marie: Yes. I usually am.

Me: So how do you think they feel about helping you if you are coming to them, looking at them, frowning, and conveying anger with them with the expectation that they should treat you well but that they will mistreat you instead? Do you think it may affect how they really do interact with you?

Marie: What are you getting at?

Me: Maybe when the other person sees you looking at them, let's say intently, glaring maybe, with anger or frustration on your face, since your expectation is that they are going to mistreat you, they may think "Oh, I don't want to deal with this person because they are going to be angry and difficult." They may look away, maybe not attend to you as soon as possible, maybe it triggers in them some of their own beliefs about themselves or the world, and you end up meeting their faulty beliefs, their own insecurities, and self-defeating beliefs, with your belief that they are going to be abusive with you. What do you think? Is that possible?

Marie: I guess. But they still shouldn't treat me badly.

Me: Where are the "should" and "should nots" written? I'd like to see that rule book. Are you saying it's ok for you to presume to know what others think, feel, and do, but they are not supposed to do the same?

Marie: Well, it's not fair. They should respect me and treat me like a human being.

Me: But it's ok if you don't do it for them?

(Silence.)

Me: I'd like to suggest that you set up the outcome of your interactions with others based upon what you believe will happen, and it all stems from your core belief that EVERYONE abuses you, that you are a victim. And maybe that belief is wrong.

I should add here that I included this brief teaching therapy episode so that the reader can get an idea of cognitive restructuring. Sometimes a picture is better than an explanation. It's the beginning step of challenging our previously constructed story that tells us who we are and what the world is like. I use this example to show how we frame what happens to us within the structure of our story, which is based upon our core beliefs.

Magic or Magik, as it was once spelled, is real. But it is not what most people think it is. It is simply the arranging of focus coupled with the precise intent to bring about an event or circumstance. Remember in a previous chapter how I talked about waking up in the middle of an out of body experience at night, how terrified I was because something was coming up the basement stairs to get me, and how I remembered Don Juan's admonition to Castaneda to shift his gaze so that the terror would disappear? That is exactly what happened. When I shifted my gaze, my mental focus also changed. The focus on terror and being gotten by something terrible went away immediately and only when I brought my attention back to my terror did it manifest again.

This is what we also do in waking life, although as stated previously, the result is slower because we are working with snail slow energy. In the dream state, we are manipulating faster vibrating energy. But for energy to become materialized into objects, such as a desk or a rock or buildings or a body, it has to slow down considerably. Then it can become physical and detectable to our physical senses. It is crystalized from waves of energy to particles.

Our physical senses form our reality. Without them we would experience nothingness. They are hardly perfect or all inclusive. We know our vision can only detect a very small portion of the entire spectrum of light. The same goes for our hearing, touch, taste, and smell. We are designed to only perceive a tiny part of the available data. Some species perceive much more of the spectrum than we do. Why is that? It is because our neurological systems are limited to a specific portion of the spectrum and everything beyond it is undetectable. What this means is we cannot trust our perceptions to define for us what is real. We can only detect the portion we are designed perceive and everything else is beyond our reach. But that doesn't mean it doesn't exist. It only means we cannot perceive it with our ordinary senses and that we dismiss information that doesn't fit within our limited beliefs about what is real.

One can safely conclude that reality, whatever it is, is well beyond our perception and what we consider reality is only a small portion of what is. The mind-blowing fact is that what we do perceive is only given form and meaning by our neurological systems and may not be anything other than a projection of our beliefs, a hologram, as previously stated.

Yikes. So, what is reality? I don't know. That is why I don't rule anything out as unbelievable. We only know what our brains can know and even that is flawed by belief and expectation, or at least formed by them.

Science is limited. Einstein said it. We can measure the room's dimensions and everything in the room. But the instruments are also of the room. The measurements are flawed, as are the instruments. They are only measures of that room and are completely invalid for measuring anything outside it. This is the basis of relativity theory. Everything is only legitimate due to its relativity to something else IN THE SAME ROOM, so to speak. Science is basically flawed in that it follows its own dogma as fastidiously as religion does. Neither of them contains "the truth". They only define their own "room" by the rules of the room itself.

When quantum physics came along and broke the rules of Newtonian physics science was dumbfounded. The walls of the room have been enlarged and we are discovering new tools. But here is the kicker. We are still in a room and still trying to define it, just with some new rules. My bet is we can never really know what the room is or how to measure it. And we can't define what God is.

Or can we?

If we step outside the story of the world that is formed by our core beliefs, such as "what you can't perceive can't be real", maybe we can at least enlarge the dimensions of our understanding.

In summary, we form our individual and collective realities with the use of our very limited perceptual systems, our eyes, ears, taste, touch, and smell. We take in data that reinforces our core beliefs which were formed in the first seven or so years of life and which tell us who we are, who everyone else is, what the world is and how things work. These things are filtered through our personalities and predispositions. Then we project those images onto the canvas of time and space through the use of hologram. Reality is a projection of thoughts and emotions based upon core beliefs. Then, ta-da: we now attribute meaning to everything in our lives based upon those things. And that is how our story forms and becomes the "truth" by which we live. It is only when we can realize this and step back from our story that we can begin to revise it to be what we want for ourselves. It is only then that we can get a clearer picture of how we create the story that we live within and change it. Then, we can begin to live consciously.

Chapter 5

CANCER

Cancer can be a great teacher. I know that on other levels of being I chose it, and that it was a result of repressing my feelings, desires, and the inauthenticity of my choices. I was living in a situation that was literally taking the life out of me. The body is the three-dimensional expression of spirit, our own little fragment of consciousness.

I had been out of graduate school for just two years when the cancer was discovered. For a year prior to that, I knew I had cancer in my breasts. I postponed getting a mammogram because I was embedded in my agony and my children were struggling. I was simply too preoccupied and busy to deal with health issues.

Denial has always worked well for me. Sometimes too well. It is the mechanism I used to keep myself in a situation which was my imprisonment…albeit one that I chose over and over again on a daily basis. I will not go into my daughters' struggles. However, I was literally consumed with worries about them. They had assumed the predictable roles that entrap members in a dysfunctional family.

Family dysfunction takes on an intergenerational pattern unless it is consciously interrupted by the individuals involved. From my perspective, my marriage was constructed after the one my parents had. Of course, it also reflected my ex-husbands upbringing. Without realizing it, I passed on my family of origin dysfunction to my own family. My ex-husband has, I'm sure, his own perspective. But the significance is that unless we are conscious of ourselves and what we are creating, we are doomed to pass generational dysfunction to our own children.

I finally went to my doctor and had the mammogram. I could see the cancers in both breasts on the films when the tech stuck them up on the light board. After the biopsies, the official cancer call didn't come until a holiday celebrating statehood. I had placed a call to my doctor's office asking for the results the day before, but he had gone on vacation for a week. I complained that I shouldn't have to wait for his return to put an end to the suspense. So, his partner ended up calling me on the holiday. I was watching the annual parade on TV, lying in my office on the futon where I slept every night at that time. He told me I had breast cancer.

Intuitively, I knew why. And I knew I would survive.

It was so clear to me when I was diagnosed that I had given myself cancer. I often had said I felt like the people in my family were "sucking me dry". How apropos and prophetic that comment was. My life was falling apart everywhere. Everything in my life was saying "CHANGE!".

I had many surgeries, radiation, and chemotherapy over the next couple of years. I had a lot of time during my recovery periods to think. I realized that my life was temporary regardless of whether or not I made it through the cancer. I had been given a 50/50 chance of recovery. However, I never felt that the cancer was MINE. It was an inconvenience that I had to deal with. I walked through treatment, just putting one foot in front of the other, and tried to hold our lives together. Fat chance. I was learning that I couldn't control anything.

I found that the way I thought about the things happening to me was of supreme importance. During radiation, I fought panic by picturing the rays zapping the cancer cells. During chemotherapy, I visualized the poison eating them like a Pac-man character. I listened to music that elicited the spiritual within me and I meditated. I focused on expelling the cancer and I never referred to it as MY cancer, only THE cancer. And then after three years of intense treatment and more surgeries, it was over. A couple of years after that I stopped the oral chemotherapy that I had been told would be a good idea for me to stay on for the rest of my life. The side effects were disturbing, and my intuition told me to stop them. I stopped the medications and never did any more cancer follow up or screening. "Nope. No more cancer for me." That was two decades ago, and I haven't looked back.

My inner voice has always been there. But I had learned to ignore it when it conflicted with my beliefs, such as the one I had that said I didn't have the right to be assertive. It was ignoring my inner voice of wisdom that led to me developing cancer. What science is now telling us is that the emotional, the spiritual, and the physical are all intertwined. I suspect like all separations, it is illusion and they are all the same thing. In our society, we tend to view them as discrete parts of ourselves rather than the gestalt of self that they really are. My breasts manifested my emotional repression and spiritual lack of fulfillment by becoming sick. And it is no mystery why it was my breasts as opposed to any other organ in my body that did get sick. The breasts are the external physical manifestations of nurturing, of caring, and they are, coincidentally, covering the heart. If I were to summarize my unhealthy emotional condition it would be to say that I was consumed with trying to keep things under control in my family, to keep people as happy as possible, and to hold everything together. Of course, I failed miserably.

Another result was that I was not there emotionally for my children, especially my youngest. She has told me she felt like I was "finished" by the time I had her. She's right. I can see the signs in retrospect, of course. But I felt helpless to do anything about them at the time. I hid away in my room, I read, I listened to music, I tried desperately to nourish myself, and in the process, I emotionally abandoned my children to their own nightmares.

My oldest daughter fared the best, even though she'd had a very difficult childhood. Maybe it made her more resilient. It is that strength that carried her through Abby's long illness and eventual death. She and her husband,

and their other daughter, have been so brave and strong. I am in awe of them.

Cancer was a physically manifested metaphor for my life. It was the externalization of the dis-ease in my life. I never thought, "why me, why cancer"? I knew why. Although I would never choose cancer on a conscious ego level, I know I chose it on other levels of myself; the larger entity that gave rise to me chose it to compel me to change. And I thank the Goddess for it and for what it taught me. I believe I had to have it to really extricate myself from my miserable life, from the marriage that I had so long considered my prison…although I didn't fully understand why I had allowed myself to languish as I had for so long. Cancer turned me inward for answers to my life, for meaning behind my suffering. The answers were there waiting for me to ask the questions.

In retrospect, I learned that my life is the only point of manifestation that I have in this incarnation. It is the point of creation that I can use to create anything I want. I thought initially that cancer taught me that since this is the only life I am aware of, and it is the only life I can consciously influence right now, I needed to move on to make this life what I wanted it to be before I died. That was part of it, certainly.

However, the larger lesson I have become aware of is that if I had stayed in my marriage, I would have been choosing death rather than embracing the lesson I needed to learn about my purpose. And that is that I create my own reality. All of it. If I don't take complete responsibility for that, I am leaving space for me to live in the default of my core beliefs which have not served me well. They were the basis of the cancer I gave myself and I knew I'd die if I didn't change. Taking full responsibility for everything in my life enabled me to change what I believed was unchangeable. It has enabled me to identify faulty core beliefs and discard them, and it has allowed me to step outside of my story of self so that I can choose to create consciously what I want. It has made all the difference.

I believe in reincarnation. It makes sense to me. It only makes sense that the life we have is just a tiny part of our overall existence. And of course, my early experience in the dentist chair had revealed to me that I am God, just as everyone is, and that we are all part of the same consciousness. I don't profess to know what is true. I don't know anything really, and neither does anyone else. But I choose to trust in my own experience, that we are all eternal beings, that we are all living in endless numbers of dimensions at once, that there is no time or space other than what we create with our physical senses, that we are all gestalts of consciousness/spirit, and that the whole which includes everything physical and non-physical is one thing. And the one is more than the sum of its parts.

Chapter 6

ADVENTURES IN CONSCIOUSNESS

GODS, REALITIES, SCIENCE, AND PERCEPTIONS

All my life I have been on a quest to understand the nature of God. That's an all-consuming task and I find myself freshly offended when someone, anyone, speaks like they know what God is and what God wants. This really perturbs me. I have sat through more church meetings and been within ear shot of more discussions where someone was saying what God wants than I care to remember. "God wants us to be happy, God says premarital sex is sinful, God intends for us to..." How egotistical of us.

For a mortal with a very limited neurological system which perceives only a tiny portion of data, to say anything definitive about God is absurd. First, there is no proof that there even is a God. Having said that, I will say that I do believe there is a creator. My experience tells me that ALL THAT IS contains the wholeness of everything manifested, dreamed, and which contains the possible, probable, and impossible. But I have no idea what ALL THAT IS, is. Is it a human looking man with a long white beard sitting on a throne in the sky? I sincerely doubt that if there is a creator of everything, it is that. And I think we are extremely egocentric beings, very narcissistic and simple if we resort to this minute construction of one.

The God of man is self-constructed, a mirror image of himself. And the reality of what is God, providing there is one, is simply unknowable by mortals. It is interesting that in every region of the world, God is depicted as the deified counterpart of the dominant person in that society. In Western Christianity God is usually a white male. In the Muslim world God is a black male. In pagan societies, the Gods and Goddesses mirrored the various influential states of the humans in those societies.

When I speak of God in this book, I will be referring to my own construction of God. It is based upon MY experience, not the experiences or interpretations of others. Remember my dentist chair experience? What I felt then on more than an emotional or intellectual level was that God is everyone and everything, is genderless, and is more than the sum of all of its parts. That God, as I experienced it, is pure and indescribable love, for a better word. Unfortunately, English doesn't contain a word that adequately expresses that all pervasive feeling, that presence, other than the overused and bland word "love". That experience of God was tangible and I experienced God as the fabric from which the consciousness of everything was woven.

To begin this discussion, I need to start with some basic concepts from science, quantum physics specifically. I am not a scientist and the descriptions I will give here are undoubtedly inadequate. Hopefully, they are mostly accurate. They will be quantum physics as I understand it. I would encourage everyone to go after better and fuller explanations of the principles I plan to introduce, which have played a big part in my spiritual awakening and development with the hope that they can help others do the same. I will blend my own beliefs and perceptions with what I have learned about the science to make my points.

As previously stated, Quanta are subatomic particles, parts of atoms so small that they can't be visualized. Their presence is detected by the influences they have on any given energy field. First, what we perceive as matter is formed from incredibly slow vibrating energy. Energy vibrates at various frequencies and when it gets slow enough, it becomes the stuff of matter. Science has shown that what we perceive as solid is mostly space, as subatomic particles have very little mass compared to the space around them.

Things occur so slowly in our reality. Our thoughts, which are based upon our largely fictionalized beliefs about the world and ourselves, organize energy into matter, although it is an unconscious process which is designed to be really poky because we are learning that it is indeed we who create reality in all of its various manifestations. It is we who determine everything that eventually is manifested in physical form, from our own bodies to hurricanes. It is we who create events. And it takes a very long time of us visualizing our goals and dreams, taking tiny step by tiny step to reach them that creates the reality that we know. But make no mistake about it. We are the creators of our reality, both within the physical realms and in the emotional and psychic ones. WE are the creators. More specifically we are THE creator.

We are fragments of ALL THAT IS. We are both the created and the creator, the dreamer and the dream. There are simply no real boundaries or divisions between us as individuals and everything else, material and nonphysical. I have experienced "God" as a gestalt of consciousness. As human beings we are fragments, personalities, fractals of consciousness manifesting in a physical form on the outskirts of that great gestalt. Imagine ALL THAT IS as a giant ball of consciousness, aware of itself, and in constant creation of experience, becoming more and more of what it is with each new creation and each new experience. Imagine the limitless layers being added continually to the ball, all being a new creation and part of that God. Imagine each new layer of that ball being made up of smaller fractals, each one a fragment of the entire consciousness, giving rise to new fractals that are fragments of it. Each new fragment having its own identity but being part of the whole and containing the whole within it. And then imagine that the ball of God consciousness gains by the experience of each tiny fractal which makes the whole increase with each new experience. Therefore, consciousness is in the constant process of creating itself and is ever changing and ever growing.

Another way to look at it is that ALL THAT IS is the body of God (not physical, but you may need to imagine it that way due to the limits of our small minds). The stomach is a discrete organ in the body with a discrete function. Although it is a complete thing, it is still part of the greater whole and cannot continue its stomach-ness without being connected to the body of the whole. And within the stomach are cells. They are complete within themselves, but again are also part of the larger whole and cannot continue their cell-ness without the stomach and the entire body. And within the cells are atoms, whole within themselves but again both essential to the whole and the whole being is essential to them. Within the atoms are quantum particles which are discrete but at the same time only valid within the context of the whole. And within the quanta are energy units, the stuff of which everything is composed, both physical and non-physical. This stuff is either vibrating quickly and forming limitless realities that are imperceptible to us or vibrating slowly enough to be used by our minds to form matter. This is called a gestalt. The whole is made up of ever smaller and more specific parts, but the whole is greater than the sum of those parts, each of which are valid and complete within themselves, within their own experience, <u>each containing the whole</u>.

That is us as humans. Think about it. We are the nerve endings of God, the creators of experience while being the created at the same time.

This was an example of gestalt in matter. The gestalt of consciousness is much the same. The consciousness of ALL THAT IS is made up of ever increasing and ever more specific units of consciousness. Each fragment or discrete unit of consciousness contributes to the overall consciousness of ALL THAT IS by providing experience and creativity. Creation and experience. That is the work of consciousness.

Within that context it becomes clear that there is no right or wrong, no good or bad. Just experience. There is no prescription from ALL THAT IS about how we live or what we do. We just continue to create and grow and experience. It's that pure, that simple.

So then where do we get our stilted small ideas of God? What is that about?

Keep in mind that we are not capable of perceiving beyond a very small range of data. Keep in mind that we are not capable of imagining very far beyond what we perceive. Keep in mind that we are limited by our sciences, our educations, and our conditioning.

When we are born, we have a plethora of DNA. There are predispositions for everything. Our genes will determine our eye color which won't likely change. But a lot of what there is about us is just a "predisposition", a possibility. Say, for example, that I am born with a predisposition for diabetes. That doesn't mean I will automatically be diabetic at any point. Rather, I may become diabetic if other factors cause my body to manifest diabetes.

The first is disposition. We are all born with certain hard wiring, like the eye color. Disposition is likely to also be fairly hard wired. There is a lot of study right now about what makes some individuals resilient when others coming from the same environment are more fragile. Disposition is the "flavor" with which we meet the world. It is our own unique approach to things, particularly stressful or uncomfortable things in our world. Dispositions range from "easy going", to "curious", to "irritable" and more.

Then there is the environmental influence. We know that for someone to become diabetic they need to have the DNA predisposition for it, but there also needs to be an environmental stressor, such as personal tragedy, poor diet, and other factors. There are a lot of very overweight people who never become diabetic. And there are people who are not overweight who do become diabetic adults.

When I was a nurse, I had a patient in his 50's who had developed diabetes. I was doing diabetic teaching with him and mentioned that a stressor often causes our body to manifest diabetes if we are predisposed to it. He then stated his son had been a drug addict for all of his adult life. The patient and his wife had rescued the son from his life, put him into treatment, paid for it out of pocket, and then their son had been released. He returned to his life, his environment, and began to use drugs again. The man had been so stressed for so long about his son and his limited ability to make his son stay clean, that it had triggered his predisposition for diabetes, and he immediately became insulin dependent. And then there was his own disposition, his personality. He simply was not able to manage the stress of the situation. He found himself trying to control something he couldn't. He crashed physically and emotionally...and developed diabetes. By the way, he was not overweight.

Of course, excess weight can be one of the stressors that can cause diabetes to manifest in someone who is predisposed. But my point is that there is a "trifecta" that contributes to anything becoming part of reality...a genetic predisposition, a personality disposition, and an environmental stressor or trigger. When it works to our benefit, such as in manifesting a dream of success in a particular area, it is considered good. When it results in an uncomfortable situation, it becomes the trifecta of God-awfulness.

When I was a young woman in my 20s, I had a dream. Remember I was miserable in the life I had made for myself, and I felt helpless to change it. I dreamed I had a choice. I could choose to become diabetic or to develop Multiple Sclerosis. I experienced agony in this dream. But I knew that it was my choice, and I was tasked with choosing one of them. I chose diabetes, as I felt MS was much worse. Guess what! I was diagnosed with diabetes at age 50. I can see now that the most lucid part of me, my higher consciousness, knew I was headed for a physical manifestation of my corrupted and mistaken beliefs about my own helplessness. As it was, I also manifested breast cancer due to the trifecta of God-awfulness: my genes, my personality disposition, and my everyday life.

As human in this vibrational medium, some of what we manifest is under our conscious control, but most is not. The task for us as fractals of the God consciousness is to become more and more conscious so that we can manifest deliberately instead of unconsciously manifesting our fears and believed limitations. I suspect that is the real meaning of life, and the only task of consciousness. To learn to manifest consciously.

Part Two

"I AM"

"When you think, choose carefully the thoughts of things you'd like to be . . . Thoughts entertained in the minds of men Become Tomorrow's objectified whims."
— *Margaret Runyan Castaneda*

And there I stopped adding to the Story part of this book. Without the structure of my STORY, other structures became plastic, and I began to experience a journey I had only been able to intellectualize about. I had dumped my old story and become story-less. When I let go of that structure a lot of other structures went with it, such as what constitutes reality and what consciousness is capable of. Suddenly, anything was possible. The deeper I went into consciousness, the more I experienced what can only be classified by most sober and sane people as weird.

In any case, there went a whole bunch of frameworks and paradigms of belief. Possibilities and my consciousness were unlimited. I started rereading the Seth series (Jane Roberts) again, Castaneda's stuff about Don Juan again, Delores Cannon's books that spanned decades working with hypnosis and experiences of consciousness from alien abductees. I reread Buddhism, parts of the Bible, Whitley Strieber's autobiographical stuff, Wayne Dyer, Dr. Andrew Weil, Greg Braden, Lynn Andrews, Masaru Emoto, and so many more. I read a fabulous book by scholar, Chris Hardy and books by Zachariah Steichen and a bunch of other stuff on the alien theory of human creation. And then I reread them. I have always had a multitude of wonderful teachers through books. It's how I learn best.

When I think back on my life and childhood, I remember so many telltale signs that I would be experiencing the expansion of consciousness that I am right now. A flood of memories come back to me. Some I have already mentioned, like lying in my back yard of my country home at night and really seeing the depth of that brilliant universe, becoming part of the universal consciousness, blending consciousness with a brontosaurus, with the red rocks over the hill where I lived. I can remember spending a great deal of time doing this, what many would call meditating now. And what happened with all this reading, meditating, and then realizing my old story had ended was that I could now design a new one, consciously, in any way I chose. I found nothing is "real", but ironically, that everything is "real".

I have always wondered and wanted to know. When I was 15, I had a patriarchal blessing. In my church, there were "patriarchs" who would give people blessings. The church was founded on fabulous accounts of supposed events, such as the founder being visited by an angel. He claimed to see God who introduced him to Jesus. I don't intend to dispute the validity of this, only to show that I had been programmed to accept the weird and unusual. What it did was make me open to experiencing things I wouldn't have recognized otherwise. When I was told there was an old man in the church whose job it was to give blessings (psychic readings), I believed it. I still believe it. I just don't believe the dogma of religion, any religion. That reading was, and still is, spot on. I have had other psychic readings, have had my charts done, have joined a numerology group. They are all very similar and they all fit me.

My religion taught that the patriarch is inspired by the Holy Ghost to give a person a blessing. My Mom and Dad drove me to an old man's house. We interrupted his Sunday dinner. He appeared a bit annoyed, although he knew we were coming. Then he laid his hands on the top of my head, said a prayer requesting a visit by the holy spirit, and went into what I now recognize was an altered state of consciousness. He gave me a reading that I reread on occasion, and it always feels correct. In it I was told that I had many "gifts and talents" and would develop more, all of them to be used to help humankind. But above all, it told me I had a specific invitation to, "ask, and it shall be answered. Seek and ye shall find. Knock, and it shall open unto you. And this is your invitation, Sister Sherry. Prepare yourself and hold yourself in readiness for the blessings of the Holy Ghost." We believed the Holy Ghost whispered to us what we should do. Some call it intuition, some inspiration. I believe it is the higher consciousness of which I am being "dreamed". "Seeking" spiritual answers has become the core around which my life has revolved, from my childish inquiries as a child to learning how to blend scientific knowledge with the spiritual experiences I have had.

There were other indicators of my predestination, too. I took a course in psychic reading at the university in the summer social work continuing education program years ago. I was stunned at the accuracy of readings that everyone in the class was doing of other members whom they had never met. I did some readings at psychic fairs. I was and still am very nervous about this ability, and of some others I have cultivated. What if I'm called crazy, made fun of, fail, or succeed? What if I'm full of shit? And what if what I am now experiencing is what I believe it is, adventures in consciousness every bit as real as ordinary reality.

I've been here before. I've had out of body experiences in dreaming where I woke up fully aware that I was out. I've known when some things are going to happen. I've had memories of other lives. Snatches that caused me to literally become dizzy. I know most other people experience these things as well. We are all able to project our consciousness and to explore and create other realities if we are open to it. But because of a very limiting social paradigm, we are afraid. We may wonder if we are making it all up. Of course, we are. We just don't realize that we are making up everything. That is how consciousness creates. It dreams or constructs. Consciousness must manifest. It uses the energetic medium of whatever dimension the fragment of itself occupies to create its reality within that vibration. Consciousness needs this constructed framework, that specific frequency of vibration, to create. Without the manifestation, and the boundaries within which it is actualized, there would be nothing new. No creation.

As I stated, after my story fell away, I was structure-less, open to everything, living completely in the moment, and still wanting to know everything. Then things began to happen. I stopped what I thought was the process of this book and began to journal furious notes that sometimes came through me so fast I would lose track of them and have to back myself up. The second part of this book will be the journal entries, with some commentary, of the time between my growth toward realizing my story was fiction to accelerating beyond it and propelling myself into the unknowable where everything is created...all experience, all probabilities, everything.

First, a word about insanity. I have worked professionally with the mentally ill a good part of my career. I was initially fascinated by the psychosis I observed. After years of listening to what these people say, I have come to believe that these are people who are blessed/cursed with having no filtering screen between parameters of ordinary reality and their unleashed ability to go beyond it. Only a person who has a good, healthy ego can venture there and hope to return. This is essential to avoid self-destructing, being unable to consciously manage crossing beyond the "veil" and returning to live in this specific manifestation. I believe that is the reason so many psychotically ill people stop taking their antipsychotics. Although this leaves them completely incapable of managing in this physical reality, the seduction of unrestrained manifestation of consciousness is so powerful that they can't resist. Many of them have told me that, as a matter of fact. Why would they want to force their consciousness into these narrow parameters of reality when they can explore the vastness of All That Is. But a person needs to be manifesting well in physical reality so they can manage the chaos and wildness of the unstructured consciousness if they are to survive in this physical manifestation.

This manifestation, this physical reality, is wondrous and marvelous. It is unique, special, beautiful, and valid as any other. The ego is the psychological structure that allows us to function within it. I have heard a lot of people bad mouthing the ego, as if it were an unwelcome impediment to an expansion of consciousness. To be sure, it must be temporarily silenced in order to explore. But it should never be disabled permanently or destroyed. It is what allows us to manifest in this dimension, and that is the reason we have chosen this reality: to create within it. If the ego is permanently destroyed, the film between this reality and unrestrained creativity is dissolved and we may never come back. I have seen many people who live their lives being serially hospitalized, incarcerated, and dying young, destitute and ill because they cannot keep their ego intact enough to return from their adventures, which often become nightmares. No one who has a still developing brain, which finishes up at about the age of 25, should use substances that will lift that veil. If they have the genetic predisposition for a psychotic illness, it may trigger it. Once broken, the damaged brain cannot be completely repaired. Even my mentor through books, Don Juan Matis, talked about people who were never able to come back from the "Nagual" (the unknown) because they didn't have a solid "Tonal" with which to maneuver back into this reality. Specifically, they didn't have enough personal power to intend their way back.

Ever since my experience in the dentist chair forty years ago, I have wanted to re-experience that feeling of perfect love, know everything I knew then, and immerse myself in it. I know that I am both the creator and the created, the weaver and the woven one, the dreamer and the dream. And after years of searching and exploring, I have been able to return there, if only for a few moments at a time. I carry that knowledge, memory, and feeling with me in my ordinary reality. I see everyone now as myself, the earth as a living entity that is also myself, and I feel compassion and love for everyone and everything. As I pass people, I silently bless them and their experience, which I realize I will embrace as my own once I am not focused in this physical reality. I am in such love with this beautiful earth, this beautiful reality, with myself, with everything that I now recognize as me.

So, on I go. I am living in the spirit of Lewis and Clark, Magellan, Sacagawea, the astronauts. I am an explorer, manifesting consciousness through this little fragment I call myself. And I am breathlessly watching and creating as I go. Sherry Griffith, LCSW

Chapter 1

ADVENTURES IN CONSCIOUSNESS

(JOURNAL ENTRIES BEFORE THE STORY COLLAPSE)

As I began to read through my copious journals to extract significant experiences for this book, I came to see my growth in a new way. The patterns of my experiences and discoveries took on a cohesiveness I had only been vaguely aware of before. Instead of random spirts of insights and meanings, I could see that there was an overarching plan of development, one that I had not consciously developed, but that seemed to be welded into my DNA as a life purpose. Instead of stumbling through my life, I could see a design. And true to that design, I had constructed a reality which would propel me toward a more complete knowing of who I am.

Humankind has always had at its basis the questions of who we are, why we exist, and what meaning there is that survives our brief and often painful lives. One of the most powerful lessons I have observed in other people as well as myself is finding meaning in suffering. We all suffer from time to time. Why? Is there a cruel God who finds delight in our pain? Is there any reason for what seems to be random suffering?

I believe I have answered those questions for myself now. And in the wholeness of consciousness, the answers are there for everyone. Everyone must find them for themselves. Outside the narcissism of our individual focus, all experience is self- designed to bring us the answers to those big questions, to the realization that we experience exactly what we need in order to propel us through our day-to-day ordinariness to enlightenment. Hopefully, this book is a helpful guide for those who are interested.

Journal Entry:
6-11-2002

My divorce was final one year ago today. It was my emancipation. I told once my ex-husband he was my Vietnam and I felt we were living in a prisoner of war camp.

For so long I wondered why I got cancer in both breasts. Before cancer, lesson after lesson presented itself to me and I failed to act on what I learned, on what I knew. I had to learn to be independent and to be alone with myself emotionally. Especially emotionally. I guess it took those three years of cancer treatment to force me to pull away completely. I just knew if I didn't leave, I would die. Through the cancer ordeal I learned that my mind and body are the same thing. There is no separation.

I had blocked energy in every chakra. I can feel myself opening more every day. My home, my garden, and my pond are the external expression of what is inside me. They are my silent, peaceful space.

I am aware that I have a life's work, a purpose that I haven't yet identified. But I know there is something, some specific thing I am to do that will be manifested to me eventually.

I can do this. I want to do this, my life. Disentangling myself from constricting relationships, constricting institutions *(the church)*, and a constricting job have brought me to this point. I've done them all this past year.

Journal Entry:
6-13-2002

(I took a trip back to my childhood town.)

I don't know why I took this trip. I don't know what I'm looking for. I have an incredible nostalgia for my childhood. I miss my dad so much. I miss my sister. I've taken this trip home before to gather the shards of my fragmented self together. I am more whole now, but I'm lost. What do I do now? What do I work toward? I'm uncomfortable being in limbo.

<u>Note</u>: I had been taking trips to my childhood home off and on for years, as mentioned earlier. One, in particular, was useful. I visited the church, school, home, and I climbed the red rocks "down over the hill" as I had as a child. At each site, I gathered back pieces of myself, fragments that I felt had splintered off. I did a lot of crying, talking to myself out loud, embracing the feelings of being the child that grew up there. I felt like my pieces were coming back to me. I could feel the correctness of what I was doing and how it was making me more whole. Gathering pieces of myself was one of the best things I ever did for myself. I realize now it was an essential piece in my spiritual journey that couldn't have been bypassed.

To heal the self, one must go into their essence as far as possible until they sense the core of their consciousness, their real identity. I knew I had felt it as a very young child, and I recognized it when I felt it again. Breaking into fragments is something we all do. Trauma, unhappiness, difficulty, living on the outposts of our experience where we come to believe reality is the story we have produced over the course of our lives all cause fragmentation. It is then that the individual must make the effort to find and embrace those lost fragments. Going home was the outward manifestation of doing that. I was able to identify the feelings, which came so easily alone there with my childhood, and to own them again.

I had accomplished a lot by the time I took this trip home. This time I realized I had found and reintegrated the fragile parts of myself that had been bruised and hurt. I had reconnected with my spirituality. I had left my marriage. My children were young adults. I was ready to take another leap forward. I didn't know it then. It seems when one is immersed in a lesson, they are not really aware of what they are learning. It is only in retrospect that the lessons become multi layered and it is possible to see a pattern, a process, and find meaning in it.

Journal Entry:
6-22-02

The longest day of the year. Today I'm officially out of the church. I am my own spiritual authority.

Journal Entry:
8-31-02

The summer is almost over. The trees are heavy; my garden is grown over. I'm going to miss my beautiful back yard. My best moments are spent on the hammock by my pond listening to the water. My peace and stillness are contained within them. I've touched every corner of them. This moment is absolutely perfect!

I still can't feel a direction in my life. Other than paying off my house by the time I retire, I have no goals. How can I justify my time? I sometimes wonder if my job or teaching or anything else really has any effect on the world. I'm not sure that anything I am doing is really helping anyone.

Nothing like the pain of watching my kids struggle. Everything in my life is forcing me to detach from outcomes. When I am able to do this, things go much better.

Journal Entry:
1-13-03

My kids have pointed out that I have resentment toward my ex-husband. What emotional leakage has been coming out of my mouth? I got my aura photographed using Carillion photography. It showed I have low energy and that my chakras were constricted. The program suggested I talk or write about my feelings. I'm not sure I can anymore. I learned to repress them and bury them deep in my body. I got to where I couldn't cry or be at all vulnerable or he would go in for the kill. Oops…there's some leakage now.

I want to give up the resentment. I want to have no feelings for my self-imposed imprisonment. I want to feel indifferent about the years I spent married. Sometimes I wonder if that is even possible.

<u>Note</u>:

I began to go through tremendous changes in my life. I had been supervising three adolescent behavioral units and teaching counseling classes at the University of Phoenix. Things were not going well. I felt my jobs were in jeopardy. What I didn't see clearly was my profound depression. One of my friends told me I was coming across as a "man hater" and to be careful. That explained the lousy comments I received from several classes I taught during that time. My kids were struggling, and I experienced more grief and agony over them than I ever did over the cancer. So, I fled. I pulled away from everyone. At the time, I believed my story and I was miserable.

As I reread the entries in my journal, I'm struck with the fact that I had a lot of insight into my misery, but it was only intellectual. I just wanted to head south and disappear, as I stated in my journals more than once. I just wanted silence.

If I can say anything about this period of time, which lasted largely from 2001 at the time of my divorce to 2015 when I realized I had no one and nothing to forgive, bringing my story to an end, it would be that while we are suffering, we cannot see the reason. We can't understand it for what it really is. I had no idea that I was the only problem in my life, that I was literally writing my story, producing, and staring in it. I didn't realize that pain and suffering were the necessary manifestations of self that would guide me into more full alignment with myself on a grand scale. I stumbled through life trying to manage things, learning how to feel again, learning to be honest with myself, beginning to pay more attention to what my thoughts and emotions were telling me.

As I began to allow myself to feel, I began to discover more things about myself.

Journal Entry:
3-31-03

I crashed yesterday. Low vibration and depression. Spent time crying. Life felt so acute, so sharp. I felt like I became everyone. I saw and felt their lives. Too much for me!

So much stress with my kids. They are struggling and I am terrified for them. Don't know how to help, afraid I'm helping too much.

I'm not always right. I must stop trying to control others. I need to allow…

Source, please be with my kids.

<u>Note</u>: Four years passed without any journal entries. My granddaughter, Abby, was diagnosed with SCIDS. She had her first bone marrow transplant but had severe graft vs host disease that nearly killed her. My daughter, her husband, and their young daughter suffered more that I could imagine over the course of Abby's illness. Her suffering was unbelievable.

After a couple of years of awfulness, Abby had a second bone marrow transplant. The donor was very difficult to find. She was an older German woman. We never got any other information about her, but it changed Abby's life from one of unreal discomfort and sickness to one of delight and joy. She began to be able to participate in the life of a normal child.

Journal Entry:
8-9-07

My life is good. I'm happy, satisfied, full, at peace. I work a lot, spend a lot of time with the kids and grandkids, care for my home and yard and have a dog named Dante. All is well. All is good.

Note: Over the next several years, I didn't write in a journal consistently. I have found pages stuck in my books, in old purses, in pockets of jackets, in drawers, and in other random places where I journaled something. Then, of course, they disappeared.

I kept reading what my spirit guides and teachers had written. I'd rotate self-help books and books on spirituality. Sometimes I'd read about alternative methods of healing. I changed jobs, stopped teaching, took stained glass classes, tried painting, worked on my house and yard.

My best male friend and I began our relationship. My journal is full of entries saying I would never have another relationship in my life. But I began to wonder if I could get close to someone the way I believed I could. I found that this relationship was very different. Before, my relationships had been all consuming. They were fired up and exciting, highly passionate, and painful. Chaos is a good descriptor. This relationship was calm, light, less consuming. It felt healthy. So, I allowed it in.

The thing that creates loss of self in relationship is the same thing that causes the relationship to be so exciting and charged. We see in the other person a reflection of ourselves, and we fall in love with ourselves through their eyes. We don't realize that of course. But once the reflection fades, we see the other person. We no longer see ourselves reflected as we did in the early stages of the relationship. And that is when the struggle starts.

It's supposed to be that way. We create our relationships in order to learn self-love, to learn about our own incompleteness and to motivate us to become more complete. Relationships which are driven unconsciously by the need to fill an empty space inside are all about this.

My new relationship wasn't chosen because our empty spaces were being filled by the other. We had, over the course of our own struggling, learned to fill ourselves. So, we comfortably took friendship to "the next level". It grew on us; we allowed its process. I discovered I like the person I am better with him in my life.

I was still reading quantum physics and spirituality, along with alternative human history. Anthropology and the uncovering of eons of advanced civilizations on this earth had always interested me. When I was a kid, I wanted to be a scientist. I didn't know what kind. But I knew I wanted to understand everything. I also knew as a kid that science and spirituality were the just different perspectives of understanding about the same thing and that the separations between them were illusion. I started journaling again.

Journal Entry:
8-10-14 (Prior to the discovery and end of my long-articulated story.)

Setting: We were in downtown Denver sitting in a public square watching people pass, listening to music, looking at the buildings stacked around us. I realized the surroundings were a construction of mine and of the others there, like a painting---artificial feeling---superimposed on and within the field in front of me.

Reality for each of us is a group participation process. Our reality is limited and produced by our senses. It doesn't exist beyond them, only the memory exists with its own reality, of course. We glide in and out of other's realities, co-creating each other and the scene together. We are the builders. We build the physical scene by collecting free energy, slowing it and organizing it into physical-ness. We all reinforce the structures that individuals produce from matter. We use the free energy from the field to re-create those formed structures moment by moment, reinforcing the structure. We just don't know it consciously. Then we move on while others continue their own process.

We glide through life doing this process of co-creation without the awareness that when we change our focus to new surroundings, the one we left is no longer in existence. That's the work of the 90% of the human brain that scientists claim we are not using, construction of physical reality.

This also applies to how we create our own bodies and assist with others in creating theirs. The individual does the arranging of the body while we all contribute to the conversion of raw energy into physical material.

(As I am typing this, I am also reading it for the first time since I wrote it. Interestingly, I put it quotation marks in my journal. Was I channeling and didn't even realize it?)

Journal Entry:
8-10-14   Later:

My perceptions are beginning to change. I can see that real art is a gamble, an experiment. Van Gough's man in a straw hat isn't beautiful, but it was new, stunning in its ability to motivate emotion. I want to paint an Indian woman on my garage and find my own style. I need to be adventurous.

Journal Entry:
9-2-14

I'm reading Convoluted Universe, by Delores Cannon. It's affected my dreams:

Dream: I went back in time to tell my daughter and son in law about Abby. I said they could have another baby and do testing at birth, enabling a bone marrow transplant that doesn't need any chemo or radiation preparation. I said it was very successful and they had a choice. My son in law sat at the table and cried. I felt their pain and suffering. I told them Abby is not gone. We just can't perceive her energy anymore with our physical senses.

I'm traveling dimensions to other realities and through time. Traveling through other probabilities that are also manifestations of my consciousness. I was fully conscious in my dreaming.

Journal Entry:
11-7-14

I meditated on the ancient architecture on our planet from prehistoric times over 10,000 years ago when our species was supposedly in the "stone age". I was reading about the massive structures and saw the pictures of grand buildings, pyramids, temples, and the impossibly gigantic blocks of stone they were made of. Each stone was perfectly fitted to the ones around it. Are we really expected to believe that they were chiseled by Stone Age humans with rudimentary tools? In my meditation, I suddenly received the knowledge that these enormous perfectly formed buildings were made by softened, liquidized stone, and hardened into perfectly fitted blocks. They were not chiseled and moved from anywhere. They were transformed in place.

The pyramids were power generators of some kind. They formed a power network around the earth, generating power for the earth and for other planets and civilizations. The material I read pointed out that they are the product of advanced engineering that we can't even match now. This from ancient humans who didn't have the wheel or writing. Clearly, human beings are not who we thought we were. The development of these advanced civilizations happened all over the globe, all over it. One can only conclude that the neat linear story we were educated to believe about the evolution and rise of humans is incorrect. So how does one explain the unearthed monuments at Göbekli Tepe where there are huge support towers with sophisticated carvings of animals not found in that area, people, beings, and insects? How does one account for the massive stone statues on Easter Island where there are no trees that could be used as rollers to move them?

Journal Entry:
1-4-15

Being with Lee allows me to be a better version of myself. I've thought about why and how, but those things aren't as important as just knowing that it is a fact. I feel more peaceful, happier, optimistic. It isn't anything he does. It is simply the interplay of his energy and mine. I think he experiences the same thing. He is a better version of himself because he's with me. It is as though my energy mixes with his and then is reflected back to me, transformed and tempered. I prefer this reflected energy to just generating my own, which is stark, too crisp, sharp, too homogenous. When my energy mixes with his it becomes fuller, kinder, softer, round, inclusive, satisfying, and peaceful.

Journal Entry:
1-9-15

Earth has been visited by extraterrestrials of many different kinds. It's a free will zone now but wasn't always. Hundreds of Thousands of years ago ETs mixed/seeded earth with their DNA and that of one or more of the hominids here leading to the development of multiple species of humans. But not all ETs are benevolent, and some came to gather and exploit earth's mineral resources. This happened all over earth, South Africa, the Middle East, Asia, Australia, Nazca in Peru, North America.

Early humans regarded the ETs as gods. They were all powerful and mighty. These early ETs were eventually expelled from earth in a heavenly war by an intergalactic counsel. It is spoken of in the 30,000 Sumerian texts (some that continue to be uncovered), in the ancient myths and petroglyphs of the Americas, in the Australian stories told by the aborigines, by the Chinese ancients, and in the Bible. The war in heaven was definitive. It was between two brothers, Enlil and Enki. And at the end earth was designated a "free will zone" by a counsel of ETs far advanced, a coalition of galactic entrepreneurs. Our current religions in which there is a savior and Satan are remnants of that eons long tussle of those two brothers, the sons of their royal leader, Anu, aka God the Father.

This mirrors the stories from the Bible that I was raised with. The names are changes and the specifics vary. But the essential story line is the same.

Look at crop circles. Why are they being brushed off or ignored? There is a relationship between them and the Nazca Lines in Peru. The similarities are profound. Nazca, crop circles in England and other parts of the world, carvings in Saudi Arabia from 12,000 years ago. They are geometric, include fractals and images. There is crop circle with a marijuana appearing leaf in the middle. Some look like dividing cells, insects, animals, DNA, and some like computer boards. They are like tattoos on the earth. The meanings are still unknown.

Currently, humanity is poised, if we succeed in resolving the problems that threaten our existence, to join the rest of the civilized galaxy. What will we choose? Self-destruction or inclusion?

<u>Note</u>:

The next entry shows that I am coming very close to identifying my story as a fiction of my own making. As I reread my journal, I can see the development leading to this discovery. As so often before, I knew on an intellectual level for a long time what I finally learned experientially. There is a difference. Knowing and the deep knowledge that comes on a higher level of consciousness are entwined, but different. It appears, at least for me, I must intellectually learn something, really understand and embrace it, in order for me to delve into the deeper knowing that connecting with higher consciousness brings. It hasn't been something I have been aware of enough to control in any way…until now.

Journal Entry:
1-10-15

I have the power to produce anything I choose in my life and all of my existences. Forever. It's all ok and safe. It's a lesson. In every single way, I create my own reality. It's all in the need to learn that I choose everything. And I can choose something else.

I chose every second of my all of my relationships. And every time I chose the same thing, I'd get angrier. It was really me being angry at me. Gotta stop now. It's ok to have chosen it. I learned I needed to be alone and become authentically me, not something someone else wanted me to be. I learned I won't make the same decisions again; I can trust myself; I will take care of myself.

I need to forgive myself for staying and going back time and time again. I carry that anger in my knees and my right hip. I carry it in my neck. The heaviness in my story causes the pain. I need to stop believing what I keep telling myself about my life. I was not a victim. I needed the lesson and knew I had chosen it. No one forced me. I decided. No one is the bad guy. I designed it for my growth. No need to choose it again.

<u>Note:</u>

Then it happened. The event that allowed me to take full responsibility for myself, my life, my choices, and give up the tired old story that was clearly not THE TRUTH.

THE COLAPSE

If you remember from earlier in this book, I had received a text from my ex-husband saying he didn't feel we needed to ever communicate again. I was hurt and offended. I had reacted with a vile text back to him. I was immediately sorry for sending it because I realized that wasn't how I felt and it hadn't been for quite a while.

I was sitting in my recliner the next day when I had an epiphany. I realized I had forgiven my ex-husband, I had forgiven myself, and the biggest realization of all…there was no one and nothing to forgive. I experienced at a deeper level of consciousness that which I knew intellectually. I create my reality, that there is no good or bad, there is no right or wrong, there is no judgement. There is only experience and we each create our own. Start to finish. All of it. Suddenly, I re-experienced some of my dentist chair experience. I had this knowing that was the same in both experiences. I was the creator and the created experiencing myself endlessly.

And that was it. I shed my story like the straight jacket it had become. And I was free.

Journal Entry:
1-12-15

I have discovered my story is just that…a story. I'm leaving it behind, the story that my misery was because of my ex-husband. I know I chose that experience over and over again, every minute, every day. I've told that story to others and to myself so many times…and I believed it. No more. I'm now story-less and trying to stay that way for a while. I sense there is something to be learned and don't want to rush to another story to fill the gap.

Flash of insight: I've done what Don Juan said to do: I have no personal history. That is what he meant by this, leaving one's story behind. I feel like the past couple of weeks I've made massive psychological leaps. I now have no personal history. It feels like true freedom.

It was just a story, not the truth. The real truth is that I created everything. The truth is that it is ok. No regrets. When I approached my day today without my story hanging around me like a heavy coat, I was a much better therapist with my patients. Everything felt easier.

Journal Entry:
1-18-15

I chose this life before I incarnated. It was supposed to be a path of helping others traverse their own paths. Although my choices and experiences were chosen by me to shape me into this person, I am also a result of those choices. I chose them to learn MY specific lesson. While I chose the lesson, the lesson also chose me. Wish I could say this clearly. I'm getting lost in my thoughts.

I mean that there were lessons for others I was supposed to help provide, some unpleasant for them and for me, some about others that I hope provided something that helped them with their lesson. I hope I've modeled raising vibration and that the path I've taken is influencing others and leading them back to source.

My energetic vibration is here to shine a light and lead others into raising their vibrations. There are many, many others like me. All of us in our own spiritual apprenticeships, while becoming mentors and teaching others on their own journeys. It reminds me of a pyramid, me following others to the top while leading others behind me. Like a pyramid of vibration from low to high with no beginning and no end, forever. Each individual vibration rising and raising the whole of consciousness.

I have found my purpose. It is to follow higher vibrations and lead others up the path I make. I need to write a book about dumping my story and finding true freedom of consciousness. I need to do it for my kids and grandkids. Maybe someone else will also be interested.

Note:

It was at this point that I began to experience things with an added dimension. I mean that literally. Without that old structure of my story, I came to regard other structures loosely. Reality was bending. I was delving into consciousness and realized that is where all the answers lie. I began to experience things that cannot be explained through the structure of ordinary reality.

I knew enough of quantum physics that it helped me to adjust to the randomness of my experiences. Quantum physics gave me the scientific explanation (although it is often beyond my understanding) that was satisfying to me which I had longed for as a child. It brought science and spirituality together and they became one. This union of spirituality and science simply states what I have come to realize on a personal spiritual level, that we create our own reality.

I'm not a scientist and I don't pretend to be one. I was raised by parents who asked for explanations for things. The mythical notion of the God I was raised to believe in was illogical to me. There were so many contradictions. That God was jealous, angry, and retaliatory. Yet he loved his creation like a parent would, was kind, and forgiving. And male. There was no female in sight. Only the quiet understanding in my church meetings of a

Heavenly Mother whom we were denied knowing anything about because, supposedly, God was protecting her from us.

I only was truly atheist for a short time until I began to believe there was a creator, but still couldn't get a good grasp on what that might be. Still a simplistic notion, but I had to start where I had left off, and I simply wanted to know more. So, I went looking.

As I stated before, I read everything I could about the subjects of quantum physics, spirituality, and how to heal oneself. Quantum physics brought it all together for me. There are contradictions with Newtonian Physics, the latter explaining the nature of big objects. But Quantum Physics is the study of the nature of particles or units of energy so small that Newtonian Physics cannot explain their behavior and it left traditional physics scratching its metaphorical head. Quanta simply behave in extraordinary ways.

There is so much to say here. But to simplify things I will just say that the most significant thing that has come out of quantum mechanics is that we are the creators of reality. The simple act of observation slows the vibration of energy allowing us to perceive it with our senses as objects around us. Our expectation and observation is what determines what we perceive.

My teacher, Don Juan Matis, said we can change our agreement with the universe. He meant we can step outside of our stories, our expectations, our automatic observations and create something else. Our intention and will are our tools. He was right.

Chapter 2

EMBRASING THE GIFTS

Journal Entry:
1-30-15

(Meditation)

Consciousness, like its manifestations, is structured in fractals. Each unit, smaller or larger, is identical to the next. Like a spiral shell, like the veins in a leaf, like the nerve paths in the brain.

We are families of spirit. We share multi-vibrational levels, overlapping strands of DNA like how atoms share electrons. DNA is multidimensional. This also creates a bonding similar to those formed by atoms. We tend to travel the dimensions of consciousness in association with these bonds. The geometry is in the DNA which we share on an energetic level with others. The shared dimensions of DNA go on and on forever. We are all one entity. There are no separations.

Relics and metals since 2000 BC have been found. Anthropologists and excavators have concluded they are associated with "the gods" of the times. There was a gold relic found in Europe from 1000 BC with engravings that look like spaceships, have carvings of planets and the solar system and a complex mathematical table plotting astronomies.

I believe I chose to be raised within my religion. It prepared me for the truth of things, which gets stranger and stranger. Only someone raised within the strangeness of this culture could be conditioned and eased into accepting these things. I'm accelerating, moving fast, trying to hang on to what it is I'm experiencing.

Journal Entry:
1-31-15

(Meditation)

Stonehenge was a circular support for a giant crystalline structure that was used by the off-planet colonists who came to earth to generate and circulate energy around the earth and to other bodies and planets away from earth. It was a transmitter of not only energy, but information. The massive stones held the crystal in the center, the outside ring was the conductive mechanism. The colonists of earth were scientists, they were miners of gold and other minerals, they were the creators of humans on this planet. The many massive remnants of advanced civilizations that we find all over the planet are proof of this. We mistake many things we discover as something else and frame them within our own beliefs. We have been given a paradigm of belief about our origins which is highly simplistic and incorrect.

That paradigm has humans evolving over millions of years until homo erectus suddenly popped into being without so much as a transition from beast to man. The colonizers were not all one thing, and they were not either the benevolent gods or the malevolent ones of our religious myths. They were human. They are our ancestors, and they are our future; they are us.

2-8-15

In the Seth Material by Jane Roberts, Seth stated that ETs are not what we think. Among other things he stated that when those entities enter our dimension, they must alter their own vibration to meet ours. When they appear to our senses, they take on an appearance that is not how they would appear to themselves in their home vibration.

<u>Note</u>:

Then I began to channel information. I didn't do anything different. But I would pull out my pen and journal and begin to write. The words would just come to me and sometimes they came so fast I had to have them repeated. It was dictation. The information came to me in a package. It would come abruptly, then stop just as abruptly. I wasn't aware of what I had written until I read it afterward. Then I was amazed. The information wasn't mine.

<u>Channeling</u>:

"When a human perceives what you call an ET, the ET must slow its vibration considerably. By virtue of this exposure, the human's vibration increases, and the human becomes less solid. After exposure, they become solid again as their vibration reduces to match the earth medium. The events from the other dimension become cloudy. Some individuals who have had contact are able to retrieve memory of it under hypnosis, as it focuses attention on memory obtained at other dimensional frequencies. It isn't that the ET intentionally cloaks the exposure so much as it is that when the individuals' vibration slows to meet the third dimension, they are unable to carry information or data that was generated from the higher vibration.

In the first part of your book, Sherry, you stated that when one is presented with information for which they have no psychological paradigms of belief to explain, they simply ignore it. There is no framework where that information will fit. This is the same mechanism that happens when one of your vibration is exposed to data from another dimensional vibration. It is largely forgotten because it cannot be fit neatly into the framework of beliefs about reality that the individual holds. Therefore, it follows that once an individual recognizes that their story is just a fiction they have created, they are able leave structures of belief about what constitutes reality behind as well. And in doing this, they open the path to new experience and information that cannot be fit into the ordinary framework of reality. They are then free to "channel" information from higher consciousness, albeit with some distortion. That cannot be entirely avoided, as the translation of higher vibrational experience into ordinary reality is not pure. It is confined within a communication where there are no symbols or words to express the experience fully.

*It's a lot like what you experience when you are dreaming. While in the dream things make sense, have meaning, purpose. When you wake, the remnant of the dream often doesn't make sense. Events are fragmented and seem disconnected and random. You have even been told by your scientists and others that dreams are simply the brain recharging itself and circulating bits of experience from the wake state. They are so much more than that. Dreams have their own reality and internal consistency. Just as the **dream of you** in this dimension has its own reality and consistency.*

Similarly, when one of you has the experience of perceiving the manifestation of a foreign fractal of consciousness you feel like the experience was dreamlike, non-real. As the soul or consciousness of the individual settles back into your current level of vibration, it loses conscious memory of the experience because it doesn't fit into the paradigm of your physical reality.

Entities are around you all the time from dimensions other than your own. You don't perceive them; or if you do, you don't really register what you have perceived. When you are driving down the street in your car you could perceive many of them, if you had the correlating vibration, and you could retain the memory if you had enlarged your paradigms of belief to allow that retention. You only have to allow it. But again, the ego feels threatened with annihilation when it perceives something so other worldly. Survival, it believes, depends upon rejecting the information. Remember the cognitive loop? (Part 1, Chapter 4) Its basic purpose is to keep the structure of the psyche intact. It does this by refusing to incorporate anything that contradicts the structure of the reality it claims as its own."

I get the feeling that I could meet those entities at some point, when I am not confined by my belief about reality. Would I be able to interact with them, or would my own terror brought about by the insecure ego drive me to run away, scream, or deny what I was perceiving? I want to know so badly, to raise my vibration, keep it high, then raise it higher. I feel like I have one foot higher and one foot stuck in this reality.

I've been reading Delores Cannon's work about the things her patients told her about other realities while they were under hypnosis. It has sparked many questions in me and helped expand the limits of the reality I'm experiencing.

When I was about 7 years old, I suddenly began to have abrupt and profuse nose bleeds. I can remember walking to church and my nose suddenly bleeding a river of blood. This happened many times, then as abruptly as it began, it stopped. I have never had a nosebleed since. These spontaneous eruptions of blood happened several times within a few weeks. As I was meditating today wondered if the nose bleeds were caused by an implant. Others who claim they were implanted with something had similar experiences.

Many of the people Cannon hypnotized talked about them. Others, like Whitley Strieber, also talk about them. Some odd objects have been found and removed.

I remember when my children were in elementary school, they slept overnight with some neighbor kids on the trampoline in their back yard. They came home the next day and told me that they and the other kids were just talking and playing in the dark of the night when an extremely bright light came over them. The next thing they knew it was hours later and they were on the trampoline wondering out loud what had happened. My daughter remembers this, as do I. But in the traditional framework of what we consider to be real, it has no place. We have talked about it only recently and she tells the same story.

Whitley Strieber wrote in his book Breakthrough that, "Because the experience is so strange, it has a tendency to mold itself to fit whatever expectation a witness may bring to it. When the mind perceives something that doesn't make sense, it imposes its own sense. Random shadows become The Man In The Moon, a flimsy accusation against a feared man becomes indistinguishable from proof of guilt." (1995)

<u>Note</u>: As I write this, more insight and information is downloading into my brain. The remarkable thing is that I realize that when I gave up on the reinforcement and maintenance of my story and discovered that all structures are merely stories of masses of people within this vibration, it became possible to allow the boundaries of reality to be more fluid. I started having experiences well outside the traditional framework of ordinary reality. Our ordinary reality is defined by our agreed upon story about what it is. Don Juan Matis suggested that to enter non-ordinary reality all we have to do is change our agreement with the universe. Is this what he meant?

I also began to understand with more depth the details of my old story and the pattern of lessons I had given myself through many incarnations. By the time I started this book, I had already had flashes of past lives. At first, I didn't recognize them for what I now believe they are. Past experiences. Interestingly, there is a theme throughout all of them. In one I was a fisherman. I went out in my boat into the ocean in the dark of the pre-morning hours, casted my net into the sea, and took my catch home around noon. I remember feeling satisfied with my life, my wife, my children. My wife was unhappy and haggard and had many children. I didn't understand her distress. I slipped on the slippery film on the rocks leading up the cliff to my home and community and fell to my death, breaking my neck.

In another incarnation, I was a dark-skinned child with black hair living in a tent with my grandmother and mother, father, and younger brother. I had to carry buckets of water from the well in the center of our village. It was so heavy and the air so hot. I was very small and had to work hard and take care of my baby brother. He was treated well, like a king. I was not. My life was hard. Then I was married to a man I didn't know. I was still very young. We lived with his parents and family. His mother abused me, made me work hard, was mean to me. I had two children, one son. When he married, his wife came to live with us as I had lived with my in-laws. I was so happy that I then had someone else in the family who I could be superior to, boss around, have do the work I didn't want to do. I saw it as my right, finally, to not be at the bottom of the lot.

I was a Greek man, short, stocky. I had dark hair on my sandaled feet. I had a daughter and three sons. My sons were my pride, along with my vineyard. My daughter was my slave, my wife was dead, and my daughter stayed with me unmarried, taking care of the home, and taking care of me. I simply expected it and was unkind to her, barely noticing her most of the time. My feeling toward her was one of indifference. Then I got old and sick. She dutifully cared for me and was very kind to me as I was dying. It was only then that I began to see her as a person with her own desires and needs. I realized her sacrifice, we became close, and I realized I loved her and cherished her. I was able to make amends before I died.

I was a four-year-old boy in the back seat of my parent's big, heavy black automobile. I was well dressed. My father was very wealthy, as was my extended family. My parents were in the front seat, arguing. My father was yelling, hitting the steering wheel, while my mother cried and cowered by her door. It was raining very hard, and we were on a winding road running along a rocky seacoast. My angry father was driving somewhat carelessly in these conditions. The car slid off the road over the cliff, and I died by drowning in the car.

Years ago in this current incarnation, my ex-husband and I were looking at some art his uncle had painted when I experienced a sudden episode of dizziness and feeling like I wasn't all there. I said something about when my husband and I had lived in California together and when he pointed out we had never lived together in California, I literally began to spin and felt so confused. I must have looked pitiful. He showed compassion for me and told me it was all right. When I look back on that moment, I remember being in both places at the same time, and I didn't feel solid. How does one explain and understand something like that using the ordinary paradigms of belief?

I believe I can't fully understand this life and the choices I made without looking at the memories I have of other incarnations. I see patterns from one life to the next in terms of my gender in each one, how I played both male and female parts, and how the roles of that gender brought new awareness. It seems that one of the themes I have explored repeatedly is being assertive, true to myself, living on both sides of oppression and observing it from the innocence of a child.

Journal Entry:
4-19-15

The truths are embedded in the myths and religions of man, the war in heaven, the decision for free will, the two sons arguing and fighting for our souls. Sons from the same man who ruled his kingdom, one a savior and one a devil. The soul is the essence of self, the fragment of consciousness within.

When we die, all we have to do to stop incarnating is to stop choosing it. Earth is an experiment in creativity. Many other species of life in the universe have the limitation of being programmed to be something, fill a role. On earth, the entities cycling through incarnations are given freedom of choice. The overall lesson is to realize we create it all. There is no God outside. God is the creator within and throughout everything.

There was a war in the skies between the two brothers and their allies. In my religion, the war was framed as being between Satan and Jesus Christ, one being all good and one all bad. In reality, the war was between the half-brothers Enki and Enlil, who had been given dominion over parts of the planet as their birthright. Their father was Anu, God the Father who became the God of monotheism. They were the creators of humankind on this earth, our ancestors. Enki helped his half-sister and consort to create humans from primates and their own DNA for the purpose, originally, of working the mines that their own species didn't want to do. They wanted and needed the gold from earth to patch the holes in their atmosphere. Ninmah was also a scientist and the primary designer of humans. Her DNA is linked to every human on earth on one of the X chromosomes. She is the source of the South African mitochondrial DNA we all carry that was recently discovered on the X chromosome. (Delores Cannon, Convoluted Universe, 2011.)

Enki had affection for his creation…humans. Enlil did not. He was jealous of anything that Enki got, including recognition and affection from their father, the king. Enki was a scientist. He wanted to explore creation through genetic modification. Enlil was a businessman, an entitled and self-centered man. He attempted to extinguish humanity once with a nuclear weapon (Sodom and Gomorrah) and once with a deluge of water over the earth (Noah's flood). Enki convinced his father and others to allow humans to survive and intervened on the part of humanity, his creation and experiment. That was when the war ensued, and the galactic counsel set earth aside as a free will zone.

The rest of the galaxy is watching us, enthralled, wondering what we will do next. They are forbidden to intervene, except if humanity attempts to destroy the planet with nuclear weapons. Many of them are mystified by us and by our ability to have emotions. They are invested in the planet and won't allow us to destroy it with nuclear weapons, as it will have far reaching ramifications for the galactic community throughout multiple dimensions. The safety of humanity is not ensured, however.

Ascension is not a literal rising into heaven. It has gained that image since the scriptures of some religions describe some chosen people who have been taken into heaven aboard ships (chariots of fire) by the original settlers, the alien humans. But ascension is really the process of increasing the vibration of energy/consciousness. It is part of the process of creation. There is no goal of ascension other than continually enlarging and expanding through the activity of manifestation at all levels of vibration. There was no beginning and there will be no end. And this is a concept that our finite brains cannot incorporate. We can accept it intellectually, but we cannot experience it in our present manifestation of consciousness.

> **"I know that old, negative patterns no longer limit me. I let them go with ease."**
> **—LOUISE HAY**

THE GREAT REDISCOVERY

Journal Entry:
8-16-15

Of course, the alien creator "Gods" are the basis of what humans have conceived of as "God", or any of the other names given to a mythical old man creator. It is the explanation for the creation of the God of my childhood and the Gods of the many human religions. The God of the Bible, the story of genesis and the God of my youth is literally a concept of humans to explain the colonizers of our planet by other humans. In other words, we humans share the same DNA of the Gods who are really just versions of ourselves. We are divine. We are the Gods, and they are us. It's all so simple, so logical. The beings who spawned us are not the creators of the earth, the galaxy, or the universe. But in a literal sense, they did create us by combining the DNA of Homo erectus with their own. 30,000 cuneiform tablets, carvings on massive buildings 300,000 years old, and every myth and religion says so.

The All That Is Consciousness is contained in all its manifestations. It is a gestalt, a pyramid of fractals. Each fractal contains the entirety of the whole, but the whole is more than the sum of its parts. It is also unknowable in its entirety. Yet, the individual consciousness is a fractal of the whole of consciousness. This would imply that the whole of consciousness can be deduced by understanding our own consciousness on an individual level. "As above, so below." It means much more than has been attributed to it.

I am coming to realize that this journey and drive to know where we came from, why we exist, where consciousness came from, what it is, how it was created, and what everything means is truly unknowable. All I can really know is that I AM. The existentialists embraced this notion. The mantra, "I think; therefore, I am," first proposed by René Descartes and then alternately proposed by Sartre as, "I feel; therefore, I am," is the best explanation of existence available to humans. It means that consciousness exists and creates, because that is what it does and that is what we are. And there is nothing more to know about existence. It simply IS. It doesn't give a single clue to what consciousness is or how it came to be. If there is a purpose other than creating experience, it is not one that I can conceive of. Maybe a larger purpose isn't necessary.

I find myself back to my original position as a child. I want to know the unknowable. Knowing that humans were a creation of other worldly humans and suspecting that there are similar beings all over the universe doesn't explain consciousness. It simply expresses it.

Maybe the All That Is Consciousness is also mystified about why it exists, what purpose there is if there is one, and where it came from. The Bible says that God became self-aware. "I am that I am." That was the response of God used in the Hebrew Bible when Moses asked for his name (Exodus 3:14). And that is all we can likely know. We are because we are consciousness.

The creator is within and without. It is all that is and it is me. I am God, God is everything, and everything is me as I was told in my dentist chair experience. And that is that. I don't know if more can be known…ever. I only know I create for the experience because I can do nothing else. I am creator and the creation. We all are.

I have come full circle. I am now the manifested archetype of the fool. (Carl Jung) The one who knows everything, which is nothing. The one who knows there is no purpose, only being. Just being. The fool dutifully toiling, knowing it is futile, that there is no destiny, no arrival, no end point, no goal, no meaning other than being. And so, I'll go on creating, being, in all of my disguises, all my parts, creating my selves, everything as I go. Becoming that which is created. Forever. I am the Great I AM.

Journal Entry:
8-22-15

I am where I began in my spiritual journey. It is the soul's journey that Carl Jung proposed beginning with being the innocent and moving through the stages of growth of the orphan, the warrior, the hero, etc. And it ends with a realization of the fool, that original innocence where we have no answers, only trust and faith. I have taken the fools journey back to the beginning, but now am aware of the absurdity of existence. It's when I let go of the struggle and allow conscious energy to flow through me that I can begin to manifest what I want…deliberately. It's so simple. So beautiful.

I am a sliver of a fragment which has temporarily turned its attention away from the All That Is Consciousness long enough to do what it appears consciousness is all about. Create just for the sake of it because there is nothing else. There is no before, no after, no reason, no purpose with which it is tasked.

I am all that there is. I have created everything and always will. There is no other thing. Everything is spirit, consciousness in various manifestations. Everything from the smallest creation, the most wonderful creation, and the most horrific creation is just another manifestation. All possibilities will be expressed. I, you, everything, and everyone is me. And I am God.

There is no other God before me. When I judge others, I am judging myself. When I love others, I am loving myself.

Journal Entry:
8-23-15

The channeling I am experiencing is happening nonstop in my daily life. When I am in a state of "grace", which I have come to regard as an ecstatic state of consciousness, I know I am the creator of everything, including myself. I simply am, and I am forever and continually creating myself through infusing my creations with consciousness.

There is something so sacred about gardening, being in my overgrown Garden of Eden, my sacred space where I can be alone with the earth. It's now late August. The plants are heavy with growth that seems to have suddenly exploded after dawdling in the scorching sun all summer. Birds are beginning to flock together and move in uniform and undulating patterns in the sky. I love touching the earth.

I have such gratitude for my ex-husband. He provided me with the learning experience I needed to provoke me to grow and find my own divinity. In the solitude of my life, I feel myself disentangling from him, from my kids, from my story and I realize I'm free. I am free to do whatever I want. I am peace, and I create peace. I am love, and I create love. I am joy, and I create joy. I am beauty, and I create beauty. I take necessary steps and let go of outcomes. I am the creator of everything and the creator of myself.

<u>Note:</u> As I read this in my journal, I am acutely aware that everything in this world seems to be polarizing at light speed. There is a drastically diminishing gray area between opposites and no one seems to be undecided on any issue. There is a strong tendency to see things in only black and white. Maybe that isn't so bad though. Maybe this is necessary in order for us to join together with like-minded people and make the vibrational leap to a higher frequency. Maybe this is the separation of the chaff from the wheat that the Bible speaks of. Maybe this is essential so that the part of consciousness that is ready to vibrate at a higher level can do so, leaving behind the part of consciousness that is vibrating slower.

I don't like that this sounds like a value judgement. It really isn't. Any level of vibration is not superior to another, just different and able to manifest in different dimensions with the medium present to it. Still, the feeling of this is palpable. The worldwide conflicts, the separations between alternatives widening, all the structures of society crumbling. It's frightening, like anything is that is new and different. But I sense it is essential for the manifestation of the world that we are going to create.

Delores Cannon's channel-ers have said that most people won't be aware of the split, the separation of some fractals of consciousness from others. They have described it as a process mostly. What if we were also to perceive it like we do light, as being a wave when it is in process and as a particle when it is focused upon. As a wave, it is undefined. It is its effects that are telling. And when an observer focuses on it, it "solidifies" and becomes a particle. What if the ascension, the move of some consciousness to a faster level of vibration is like that? The focus of everyone is flowing in process to an ideological transcendence as individuals and groups can pause and focus, freezing the effect of flowing consciousness to affect its direction and manifestation. We change the flow by our focus.

This has far reaching implications for those of us who are engaged in dreaming and creating the new world as the old one crumbles away. With our focus, we can change our reality. It is imperative that we have a sharp vision of how we want this new world to look, how we want it to function, and what we want to manifest as a critical mass.

I have detached from mainstream media. It is owned by a handful of entities who benefit from the labors of the masses, and the media only shows us what those entities want us to know. The media tells us what to think and how to think. I believe that it is necessary for us to stop paying attention to media for us to develop that clear vision of what we want for ourselves in our new world. Once detached, the individual mind is not polluted by the dogma that is continually being fed to us, which we incorporate and accept. Then, of course, we create our reality based upon the structure that the media has hypnotized us to believe. The media feeds us fear. What I have found is that the world is a much more peaceful place when I detach. I am more peaceful. And I generate more peace.

Journal Entry:
8-29-15

I've thought a lot about my story. My sisters have all stated they didn't feel loved by my parents. I don't feel I was not loved. However, I still had issues. They were more created from enmeshment with my parents than from the abandonment my sisters felt. Of course. My role in the family required enmeshment. And it provided the framework for my story. (Enmeshment is the psychological and psychic entwinement with others and self. One could say that it is the inability to separate the self from the other. It is the dysfunction I struggle with through my children.) Odd that so much of becoming enlightened has to do with realizing there are no separations. Yet it is necessary to separate one's energy to allow others to make independent choices and follow their own paths to enlightenment. It is also necessary to do this to take full responsibility for the reality we create for ourselves.

It's a lovely paradox. Like all truths, it is not just one thing appearing one way. It is multidimensional.

I learned to be stingy with my energy and to mindfully share it. Otherwise, I allow others to drain my vital energy. This continual leaking creates conflict between people, it creates weak children who cannot manage their own emotions, bitter parents who sacrifice essential parts of themselves in the belief that they are being good, selfless people. Everyone loses. It's my default energetic pattern.

Suffering of any kind is designed to move us closer to alignment with our higher selves.

Sitting here in my backyard Eden listening to the birds, the neighbor over the back fence talking to her dog, the perfect air, the end of summer sky, the overgrown green, and the trickling of my fishpond, I am At One with myself. It feels like atonement.

I had to sacrifice myself to the thing I call my life, then grow through suffering beyond it to see it for what it was so that I could complete the atonement. Self-forgiveness for poor choices, for inadequacies, for self-abuse so that I could find the way back to SELF AS GOD.

Journal Entry:
9-20-15

Everything is a fractal of something else. This includes consciousness. This conscious energy manifests in fractals at every level, spiraling backward and forward in every direction through the past, present and future. There is no beginning and no end. The implications of this have not been discovered yet, rather they have not yet been conceptualized. But when conceptualized they will also be manifested automatically, and something big, something magnificent is going to happen in that moment of conscious awareness and deliberate manifestation. Perhaps dissolving of the big story of this physical reality. Evolution into another dimension? Is it happening right now?

Physical reality is a fragment of the continuum of energy unfolding and refolding in fractal formation. Our physical senses pick up impulses of energy and our brains interpret just a fragment of the continuous waves of information, the part that fits into our already established beliefs of who we are, who others are, and what is real. We perceive this as reality.

All realities exist simultaneously. All patterns are infinite, and fractals of those waves of conscious energy that we can perceive constitute what is real to us, while those infinite fractals of conscious energy that we cannot perceive are either dismissed as nonexistent or not considered at all.

Energy doesn't "have" consciousness and consciousness doesn't "have" energy. They are the same thing, a building block with infinitely smaller and larger building blocks of conscious energy. Neither is separate from the other. One does not determine the other or define the other, because they are one thing.

I'm on the front lines of the rolling increased vibration of consciousness. In the world and on a psychic level I am not the first, but I'm one of those creating maps for others to follow. My input and leadership are important to the overall progress of the movement to tip the scales with a critical mass to the transformation of the earth into a higher frequency of vibration. The new world. We recently crossed the line of the psychic pathway of humanity into uncharted territory. Let's see how far we can go this time. It's time to openly acknowledge other galactic life and to take our place next to other dimensional societies.

I'm so grateful to be here, now, who I am. I get to participate in the evolutionary jump of consciousness. In twenty years, everything will have changed more than it did in the prior twenty years. It will be the new world. And I get to be one of the sculptors of it.

I have asked myself all my life about what love is. I love who I am within my current relationship. I'm authentic even though it isn't always easy. I realize now I couldn't love my ex-husband because I felt I couldn't be authentic within that relationship, and I didn't love the inauthentic self I became with him. Being single (for 10 years after my divorce) allowed me to relax into my own authenticity. And now that I know what that is and have discovered that I love that authentic self. I have become even more of who I want to be.

Love, the way it is presented to us in society, is narcissism. In relationships, we see ourselves through someone else's eyes. We see and fall in love with our idealized selves. When the illusion wears off relationships fall apart, often hatefully. We blame each other for not being able to maintain that illusion as we each fall into disillusionment. We fall out of love with each other because we fall out of love with ourselves within the relationship. In healthy relationships, authenticity is not only allowed, it is imperative if the relationship is to persist. There is very little, if any, illusion when there is an authenticity in the partners of a relationship.

Journal Entry:
11-1-15

The Biblical resurrection has a basis in the ordinary reality of this world. It is a phenomenon that happens periodically, I want to say about every 10,000 years, when those who have raised vibration ascend in mass to the vibrational level of the "gods" who made us 300,000 years ago. The ancients left knowledge of ascension in stone, a secret code, in the effort to help those who ascend in the next wave. A new one is beginning now. Is this "the second coming" of Christ? It will be another coming of those entities and when those of us raise our vibrations to meet theirs, we will be able to perceive them.

We weren't wiped out as a species in the many times before when we were on the brink of ascension or destruction. Those who were ready did ascend. Those not ready didn't and went on to redevelop civilization again. We don't know how many times this has happened. However, entire cities have been found with one build on top of the other at Göbekli Tepe in Turkey. Several layers of cities have been discovered at this site and only the top two have been excavated. Each layer that is uncovered is not only much older than the layer covering it, but it also shows that the society of the older ruins were much more advanced than the upper levels. The massive and elaborately carved stones and gigantic T-shaped pillars are more than 12,000 years old. Science tells us they are older than the invention of agriculture and even pottery.

Clearly, the theory that agriculture led to civilization is incorrect. It appears that it is the other way around; those who brought civilization to earth brought agriculture with them. Yet, the same old history of humans that I was taught 50 years ago is still being taught in mainstream schools. I would think a discovery of this magnitude would be heralded in the media and textbooks would be rewritten. It feels almost conspiratorial that with this evidence and all the evidence from pyramids and other structures all over the world the media isn't shouting about it. Why is this information being ignored? And how do we account for the other contradicting evidence that is being compiled? Is our science so dogmatic it won't incorporate it? Are our religions so threatened that new evidence is ignored or relegated to myth.

Journal Entry:
11-7-15

We are all immersed in a matrix of falseness. Reality isn't real. Death is simply waking up from a dream and seeing a larger picture of what IS real. It's both comforting and scary when it's not padded with myth and deception. I have mixed feelings. I want to know and I'm afraid to know.

There is no larger meaning. Meaning involves belief and judgement, which are part of the story and fictional too. It's all artificial.

Journal Entry:
12-10-15

An enlightened critical mass is changing the trajectory of our species and the earth. Although the work isn't done, I don't feel we will completely self-destruct.

This morning I'm full of gratitude and love for the earth. I love her. The animals, birds, land, oceans, clouds. I am everything and everything is me.

Consciousness and manifestation are never separate. The manifestation IS the consciousness. They are the same thing. Only in our humanness have we declared them to be two different and separate things. Regardless of vibration, consciousness can't exist without manifesting because its only function, reason, and purpose is to create.

Journal Entry:
12-20-15

Nothing is what we think, especially the meaning of things. Essentially, nothing means anything, and experience is just experience. None are more or less important.

I can't save the world by focusing on the horrors of climate change, wars and brutality, corrupt governments, and hatred. I've come to realize I can only "save" myself. By that I mean the only way out of the cycle of reincarnations is ascension: raising the vibration of my tiny fragment of consciousness that I call myself while drawing up the larger consciousness in the process. I have discovered how to do this. It's through mindfully living in gratitude of the beauty of this world and for the people and love I have in my life.

Consciousness grows like an ice crystal, starting with a single point, and growing outward, each fragment repeating the pattern of the larger fragment. Each fractal contains the whole.

What will this little fractal of consciousness I call myself turn into as my vibration increases? I can't even imagine; but if I can learn more about this fractal, it should be indicative of the next level to come. Yes?

Journal Entry:
1-1-16

I'm feeling desperation for the earth and humanity. We're so close to extinction. It's difficult to feel hopeful. I've been inspired lately to understand that everything "out there" is a projection of thought, of consciousness, flowing through this little fragment I call "me". The universe isn't outside me; it is inside flowing outward. I know everything can be and is possible if I allow it to flow unimpeded through me. There is no other reality.

I must focus on the objective and not on the horror, even though the horror is loud and big. I feel fragile and alone.

I'm the hero of my story. Nothing in my life exists apart from me. I'm treading on the edge of what is often perceived as insanity. I am alone in this. Everything is just illusion, a projection of consciousness through my physical apparatus. I have chosen this reality. I believe that I can choose it to go any way I want. So why is it so hard to do? What's the point? Is there a point?

I Am, and there is no reason. I exist and am self-aware, and there is no reason. I am God, God is everything, everything is me. There is nothing else, no larger purpose, no reason. Just being.

Journal Entry:
3-13-16

Thoughts of a woman who is blessed to receive almost continual insight, knowledge, and inspiration…and thinks, "I should be writing this down", but often doesn't. So today I'm writing stuff down as it comes to me randomly.

I'm sitting in my beautiful back yard at the house I love enjoying a very warm, early spring. It got warm in February, and I noticed the globe willow trees with the ends of their branches waking up and becoming pale green. Today I'll enjoy what could be the last year of my life, of the world as I have known it.

We've been warned about this time. It is both thrilling and sinful to sit here, basking in the effect of global warming. Wonderful, horrible, colossal things are coming. They are beginning and becoming more intense every day and we don't have long left before devastation on a huge scale everywhere in the world will cull many, maybe most of us, and the rest will be plunged into a reality so foreign we could be reduced to cave men again. We will still be dependent upon our creators, the "more evolved" siblings from other worlds, other dimensions. They will again tinker with the genetics, the blending of theirs and ours in an attempt to create a superior hybrid of the billions and billions of life forms in the endless universe of consciousness.

As sparks of the All Consciousness we are intended to blend, reshape, and re-define experience. No experience is invalid or expendable because every spark is All That Is.

I am making progress in understanding and knowing the creator behind the created, both being who I AM and everything in One. The limited perceptions of our physical manifestation really is deliberate. We need to not know everything in this incarnation so we can create something new, something never before created. Our limited perceptions which define our reality cause us to forget who we really are. Our goal is to reconnect with all fragments and know we are the creator.

For something new to be created that has never been explored before, the big "reality" has to be forgotten to generate creativity, rather than reproduce what is already created.

Where are the boundaries of consciousness? Vibrating just beyond me is the dreamer of me. That entity is also generating many other fractals as well. Then beyond that consciousness lies a greater creator vibrating even faster, and beyond is another cluster of consciousness, then another, then another endlessly.

I used to spend a great deal of my time as a child and teen being alone and letting my mind travel through consciousness. I felt my dinosaur-ness, being the beautiful blue white dotted sky, the ocean, or a foreign planet, or just flowing through the space of consciousness, experiencing eternal manifestations in a quest to create. That is all I can know as Sherry. It might not feel like enough. I'll always want to experience the ALL more.

There is no outside creator. And one becomes more aware of this by traveling through one's own consciousness. That is how we will be able to time and distance travel, both being a parameter of this specific vibrational reality. At other levels of consciousness, they are irrelevant. Once we realize that, we can do both at will.

We will learn to increase vibration to travel to other levels of self. We think of ourselves in 4D. But we are in multiple dimensions at once. We can travel through consciousness to places in this world, universe, and many other dimensions. Like the Tesseract in "A Wrinkle in Time" (Madeleine L'Engle, 1963), consciousness can slide through dimensions, manifesting in each reality using the manifestation laws of the dimension it finds itself within.

Energy is the medium of manifestation within this specific vibration. The thought form, or the thought manifested, cannot be split into consciousness and manifestation. They are the same thing.

The environment will change dramatically. The magnitude of suffering, unimaginable. And those of like vibration will manifest together their reality. I guess the trick of manifesting what one wants is to stay focused in the present and be aware of what this reality really is. That is how to create deliberately, more consciously. I am feeling on a very deep level that since I am creating all of my experience, I really am in a literal sense responsible for the starving children, the brutality, the wars, the anger and meanness, the exploitation. I can create something else. I think I'm learning how to do this.

If I want a peaceful world, I need to manifest peace in my own reality. If I want love, I must manifest love in my own reality. *If I want anything, I must become it because that is the basic layer of manifestation.*

For those who are ready, there will be peace and love and consideration. We will realize our part in creation and that we are all one consciousness. It will require a revolution in thinking and everywhere around me there is evidence that this is taking place.

All possibilities will be manifested. The Sherry ego will exist in all those probabilities to some extent. And humanity, along with the earth and every one of its parts will continue to evolve. It could be that climate change is required to transition us to another cycle in consciousness' evolution. It pushes us to take responsibility for what we are creating, which increases the vibration allowing consciousness to ascend. I suspect it will be less of an event and more of a gradual process with its Ah Ha moments of awareness.

Journal Entry:
3-18-16

Faith. It is the absolute belief in something. It is the law of attraction. What we imagine, either out of joy or out of fear, we will manifest. It is precisely what we fear that we manifest first, because if we are fearful, it is usually where our focus resides. And like a wave of light, when we focus our attention on something, it becomes material.

Note:

Many of the journal entries I made were of a personal nature. Because they talk about my struggles with other people, my children mainly, I am not including them. But I will say that in focusing on my own fears about them, I was manifesting the fear for myself. The interplay between individuals and the situations they create is complicated and I don't pretend to understand all of it. But I have discovered a couple of things.

Once I let go of holding tightly to my core beliefs about being responsible for everyone's happiness, once I decided to be aligned with my higher self, I realized what I had to do. I had to detach completely and pull my own energy back in. I had to allow others to create for themselves their reality and trust that their higher self was at the controls. I found that when I am consciously managing my thoughts and my focus, I can experience what I want. I become more accepting of others and less controlling in a futile attempt to prevent my fears from coming true.

I discovered I was creating the very thing I didn't want in my relationships. This was new territory for me. Pulling in my energy and blocking others from attaching to it has made all the difference. I have faith that everything is as it should be, that everything that is being manifested is for my growth and is designed to bring me back into alignment with my higher self. When I realized I was getting in the way of that, I could change.

Journal Entry:
3-20-16

Far from being alone in the universe, our solar system and our galaxy and our universe and all universes are teaming with life in every possible dimension and expression of consciousness. We are the nerve endings in the great body of consciousness, creating and being created in limitless manifestations, enabling all consciousness to expand.

Journal Entry:
3-21-16

The first day of spring. I wish words could carry the same depth as my knowing does. But words are inadequate.

Global warming is not primarily man made. Not that we haven't done our share as a species to trash the planet and kill much of the life on it. The world is getting hotter, but not entirely because of us. We do contribute, and humans have overrun the earth and destroyed much of it. The Long Year Cycle of the Mayan Calendar demonstrates that our earth position, the position of our solar system in the galaxy, and our galaxy in the universe is creating a fundamental change for earth which is affecting the climate. A planet some have named Niburu (and maybe a whole other galaxy) is crossing our path. The earth changes will be more rapid and dramatic now. It will become very hot and the face of most of the earth will bake. The oceans will warm fast and as polar ice melts methane will be released into the atmosphere. Land will become submerged. This could happen in a flash bringing on the next ice age to cleanse the earth. The terrible freezing from the release of methane will kill most surface life.

But there are those few with more of the creator's blood who made us in their own image, who can suppress information largely by claiming those who talk about the truth are into conspiracy theories. They distract us with wars and with blaming the entirety of climate change on human activity. So, why would they want us distracted?

We are mongrels and have the old slave blood in us. We are the descendants of the workers of the South Africa mines, the species created by the creators to serve them in the most literal sense. We serve the most pure-blooded ones, the ones with the "royal lineages" from the creators who interbred with the hybrid humans they created.

Our system, with a few getting and gathering all the wealth of the world, is slavery for the rest. These few obscenely rich people are suppressing scientific knowledge by the general populous to keep us ignorantly slaving away. A "black budget" is building underground bunkers the likes of the ones found in the ancient ruins in many countries, huge underground cities where survivors lived once before in the last ice age 12,000 years ago. They are stocking up on wealth and supplies in the underground bunkers the size of cities. They know what is coming. (Remember this is my journal entry. "They" refers to the forces that work in opposition to enlightenment.)

Journal Entry:
3-29-16

Relationships are the perfect mirror. Like quanta, personalities change by the observation of and interaction with another. We can, if we are paying attention, identify what we like about ourselves and where we fall short of who we can be. My only purpose in life now is to form who I want to be. My only desire is to share myself and what I know, to genuinely guide someone with a gentle light touch that will give them new perspectives that may change their lives and open them to their full creativity.

Infestation. I killed an ant on the wall by the stairs. I knew my life was no more important that its life was. I killed it, a part of myself, because I don't want them invading my house anymore.

Consciousness cannot NOT manifest. (I know, a double negative. It helps augment my point.) They are the same thing and, therefore, The Creator God is also the creation. The "aliens" are us as well as our creators. Ascending spirituality is the raising of the vibration of consciousness, and as it goes it manifests along the way in the medium of that specific vibration. Consciousness cannot be separated from its manifestation. There is no one and the other. They are the same thing.

I am beginning to experience times like in the dentist chair where I know all of this on an experiential level. The way through to other dimensions and realities is by going deeper into self…not out of body…not through what we've been told is time and space, but by going deep within. Sometimes I feel like I can be there all the time, where all questions are already answered, always experiencing the oneness of everything that is me, is everything, is God. The I AM.

I am the raven flying through the red rock arches and towers, swirling, pumping hard, then coasting and swirling some more. I am the sea lion, the trees, the desert, the ocean, the sky, the earth, the solar system, the galaxy, always evolving through consciousness by turning inward. I am God, God is everything, everything is me, and the substance of all manifestations is love. I love this world that I am creating.

The beauty of this manifestation is astounding. At some point the culling will begin, the earth to bake, starvation and lack of water on a massive scale enabling only the wealthiest and most powerful to survive.

But right now, the air is just a little moist and crisp, the breeze a bit chilly, the sky gray and overcast with the suggestion of blue sky at the horizon. I feel grateful.

Journal Entry:
4-8-16

I became everything today. I was watching myself jogging, shoveling dirt, riding my bike, barking, flying in the sky, moving through the world, watching myself in all of my manifestations. All the answers are within me. And I will know. All I have to do is ask and the answers will come. I am the answer.

I'm getting to where I can slide back and forth between worlds/dimensional realities easily, always aware of where "I" am on that continuum. I can operate at whatever level is necessary at that moment while carrying the BIG REALITY within me all the time. I can even feel different levels of myself laughing at the reality of another part, and all parts laughing together endlessly.

The key to going deeper is gratitude, Gratitude is the way, the truth, and the light. No one becomes the "I", the ONE, any other way.

Journal Entry:
4-10-16

This is it. I have what I have envisioned for myself for so long, total freedom to be myself in this little old house that I love. I am there, the place of my dreams. I feel such gratitude to be a witness at this specific time. I am in awe of who and what I really am, the architect and artist of everything from this little reality all the way up to where all is one, and it's all "I".

Journal Entry
4-17-16

Whatever happens I will acknowledge all of it as the experience I have chosen on levels of higher consciousness. I not only agree with everything in my experience but am creating what will come, me and the rest of ME, which is all of humanity. I will adapt and try to help others understand, to be one of the ones to lead the way while following in the paths of others. That will be the focus of my life's work from now on. "I once was lost but now am found." I have chosen to be a witness, a participant, a creator of the now unknown.

I am so grateful to be witnessing this big reset, if that is what it is, the evolution of it all. I wanted to be here, right now, as a guide and a witness to absolute transformation of consciousness.

The earth is going through her own growth, her own cycle of cleaning herself, healing herself. She is heating up. She is menstruating.

Spring is here. My yard is bursting into bloom, the woodpecker is tapping, birds everywhere are getting active after a rather wet, cool week. My flowers are planted. Hopefully, I can plant the vegetables soon.

I feel around me the thinning out of things. Some others do too. But so many people around me act like climate change isn't real. Media controls everything. It lets us know what the monied want us to know. Just like our own personal story, we are buying into a fiction based upon a few core beliefs fed to the masses. It is easy for the rulers behind the scenes to make war in other countries, to paint the "other" as less than "us", to compel us to fight and die. Somewhere else, while our attention is on this trumped up conflict, resources are being stolen by them…the shadow ones who are the richest in the world. They manufacture and sell arms to both sides of the contrived conflict and chortle at us nonsense about nationalism. They play on our tribal instincts.

They want us to believe we have created climate change while denying its existence. We have certainly polluted and destroyed the earth. And there is no question that our practices are destroying the atmosphere, leaving us all the more unready to deal with the baking of the earth and subsequent ice age to come. The fact is our earth is entering a part of her cycle where she is vulnerable to our sun and other forces leading to global warming. We are being distracted on purpose with an argument of whether or not climate change is happening. We are being distracted on purpose with conflict between groups of people who have different Gods, who are true to their tribe. They are happy to have us kill ourselves off, as long as we keep generating more wealth for them. They, however, are preparing. Not for humanity, but for themselves.

Something is coming. It could be a comet, a sudden methane release so fast it triggers an instant ice age, it could be Niburu and the "second coming" of our alien creators who mingled some of our primate DNA with theirs, something probably prevalent throughout the universe. Maybe all of the above.

As Niburu gets close they will reveal themselves to those who can perceive them, and our race will join the galactic community. They will show up in plain sight because we have raised our cumulative vibration to their frequency, not because they have decided to show themselves to us, but because we have chosen it. What will we choose? Will we ascend or fall back into the experiment and start over so that we create something different.

Journal Entry:
4-19-16

The earth is sick. Of course, she is. We have sucked her dry, cut her, poisoned her, then left her to rot. Whether it is the galactic cycle or manmade, global warming and species extinction is happening. Is it retribution from mother earth? But like the wise parent she is protecting herself from us. I feel her sickness all around me. Things feel less dense, as though a massive amount of consciousness has left the planet. I feel the absence of plant and animal lives that are now extinct or becoming extinct.

It's bleak. No other way to put it. I embrace the opportunity and need to help others embrace the spiritual consciousness of the moment and use it to propel ourselves into ever higher vibration.

It is an opportunity for transformation. The chance to ascend. As the spectacle unfolds, I hope I continue to do honor to All That Is, and do it well.

The call of my soul is to do something valiant.

I love the way my tulips unfold in the sun, and in the evening close up again. They are alive here with me. We're experiencing this together. The birds are bedding and quieting down. My dogs are barking me to distraction at the dogs on the other side of the fence. The air is cool, and things are greening up everywhere. What a perfect moment this is. I'll appreciate it and focus on gratitude for all of it and for being a witness. Every day I feel the oneness of All That Is.

Journal Entry:
4-20-16

I walked around my yard and blessed and loved and appreciated it. It was a connection of consciousness between me and the plants. We had an energy exchange and I experienced us becoming an extension of each other's energy. It's glorious spring. My tulips are stunning in their beauty and colors. The daffodils are so beautiful next to them. And the birds are eating from my feeders. Such a variety of birds. There are finches primarily. There are doves, crows, magpies, a blue jay, but still no robins. Tomorrow the temperature will be in the 80s.

We are all here, living specks of consciousness in all our beauty and perfection, here together to be part of this cycle of consciousness. It's ascension time. I love this world. I love my life. All of it.

Suddenly my back yard is in chaos. The birds are fighting, driving each other away from the food and their nests. The dogs are compulsively barking and chasing the birds.

I just saw a robin! Thank you, Universe.

Journal Entry:
4-30-16

Sitting here in my chair in my quiet house by myself. There is a fierce wind blowing. I suddenly became fully aware of how I have created everything and everyone in my life, I imagined them, dreamed them, I manifested and materialized them, and in that instant of pure manifestation, I let go of them so they can go their own way manifesting as they go. All of us have been dreamed by an entity into manifestation. I was the creation and the creator all at once. I get it, again, on an experiential level. There is only "The One", the All That Is. And it is me.

I am awake. I know the answers to all of the questions I've had all of my life. I know who I am. I feel what God is, what everything is. It is me. I am the answer to all my questions. All answers are within me. I only must ask, and I will be answered. I'm getting to the point of spiritual experience now where I'm having real difficulty framing what I know into words. Words have always been inadequate to describe spiritual experience. Right now, I can barely express anything even close to what I am experiencing.

I'm meditating daily and feeling such gratitude for this wonderful experience. When I allow myself, I experience being All That Is, even if just briefly. My life is a continual meditation. I am everything around me. I have created everything in my experience. Knowing this, I feel such love for everything I've created, all that I am; such gratitude and love for myself, my body, my relationships, my home, my world, my earth. I want to lovingly care for everything. Even housework is a joyful meditation of caring for my creation.

Journal Entry:
5-2-16

Cancer is on the rise. It appears to me that it is the damage we have done to the earth that is causing it all. Humans have become a literal cancer on the earth. We kill the good stuff around us and devour everything as we go. And we multiply exponentially. We have all contributed to the malignant growth we have become on this beautiful living organism.

Resources are scarce and becoming scarcer. War is increasing, hunger and poverty, cruelty and exploitation and our never-ending destruction of life.

In her desperate need to survive, earth will let us die. And she should. There is no way we can eradicate cancer within us as long as the cancer IS us.

What will her surgery look like; what will her radiation and chemotherapy be? Everything is a fractal of something identical to itself. She will excise us, poison us, burn us out of her. The way to cure cancer in us is to become benign to her. Humanity will only survive if we love her as ourselves. She is us, we are her, we are all one consciousness. She is fighting back. We have left her no choice, and she will win one way or the other. Despite all our proud intelligence and our very human arrogance, she has the upper hand. She will eliminate as many as needed for her to survive.

Still, I want the suffering of people, animals, plants, air and water to stop. I want people to love each other and all of creation as themselves. I want peace. I want us to learn from this and ascend higher. I'm watching the suffering. I'm no longer suffering myself, although I'm aware of all the suffering. I am living more and more mindfully. I follow my senses, and I see such beauty around me. I become everything.

I am so full of gratitude for my life. I am, and all I want to do is care for my creation, love it all. Be it all. Worship it all.

I feel lighter, like I am vibrating faster.

Journal Entry:
5-3-16

Came home from work and went to my yard. I was mowing the lawn and I time traveled. I visited me in the dentist chair 40 years ago. I witnessed the agony I had felt continually over the disastrous and painful life I had created. I felt my past-self escape. I felt love for her/me/everything. And when it was time, I told her to go back to her life, keep growing, keep struggling, keep looking and asking. She felt the love and marveled at how grand, vast, whole, complete, and unutterable it all is and how the love we feel as mortals is so limited and incomplete. As much as we love our children, it doesn't compare to the love of All That Is.

My past self knew for a moment who she was. She knew there were no questions, only answers. And when she felt herself being sucked back into "reality", she begged to take something back with her. "I" told "her" what I now know and experience in my life every moment. Eminence. God is everything. I told her to remember this and how it felt to know this so that she could recall it to help her get through the tough spiritual growth she would face to get back to this oneness experience…where I am now, so happy, loving my creation, becoming one with my creation on ever deeper levels.

I love for and care for all of my creation, from the routine in my job, to my home, my art, my relationships. I want to honor my creation in everything I do. I want to care for all of it. I am the eternal fabric of love.

Journal Entry:
8-16-16

A call to all ages of women: We are the women of the new world that is coming upon us so fast. We are the ones who are left. That's true of now and will be true of those women left when we are gone. Everything is changing. Everywhere. Across the world, humanity is on the brink of a most marvelous transformation of mass consciousness. We are ascending. It's not going to happen all at once. It is a process; one so perfect we can't even detect it until it reaches a specific accelerated vibrational threshold. Then hold on. Because it begins to accelerate by manifesting as a cascade of change. And the people of the earth are certainly experiencing change on a colossal scale.

The best part is that as we ascend individually, we take with us those other fragments of the God consciousness whom we have helped to raise their own energetic vibrations. We ascend together. Then they pull others up with them, and they lift others, on and on forever. We are the creators of the new world because we are here for the rebirth.

Do you feel it? Every social structure we have lived within is crumbling. That's a good thing. A very good thing. We, fragments of the All That Is

Consciousness, chose this time of transformation to be here right where we are, right now. We have helped create it and now we need to step up, take the fullness of our creative power and create the new world ahead of us. We can't afford to passively stay in our places. Not this time. We either continue to create the status quo oblivious to our role in it, or we create something new, something more functional than the old structure it is replacing.

It is our time to do the dreaming and imagining. In allowing ourselves to dream exactly what we want for ourselves, we create it. We create peace in our lives when we create peace in ourselves. When we create it in our lives, we create it our world. We draw the vibrations of others to sync with ours, leading them to be more peaceful, and in turn they lead others.

It's our time as women to do the dreaming and create structures that will be more peaceful, more loving and fair, more fulfilling, more beautiful, more wonderful. All we have to do is do it.

Calling all women: Raise your vibration. Ascend.

Journal Entry:
8-19-16: *Channeling*

"You, all of you reading this, are just one version of yourselves, of your choices, in a single universe. But you are really spread across multiverses with you in each one manifesting as a different version. All probabilities are manifested according to their vibrational strength. The numbers of your existences in the multiverse are limitless. All of them creating new versions of themselves in an unlimited number of universes.

The fractal of the Sherry consciousness allowing this psychological expansion necessary for our communication can raise your vibration. You know how to do this. Simply look at the wonder and beauty around you and allow the love and gratitude that comes with the emotion of witnessing/creating something so magnificent. As you raise your vibration, the multitude of other versions of you in all the multitude of universes is affected. Their vibrations are influenced by yours…and yours by them. The S Fractal of consciousness is raised, each of its fragments co-creating together, vibrating at ever higher levels, and lifting/being lifted by other conscious fragments.

Consciousness can "travel" in any direction that you can imagine and in unlimited number of ways you can't. In your terms, consciousness can move forward and backward in time, from one sentient being to another, it can combine with other consciousness or even join with others and go along for the ride. You think of things in discrete terms. For your solitary ego to imagine the combinations and playfulness of consciousness is impossible. It simply cannot perceive the fluidity and the memory of every combination it has ever taken. Every identity will last forever, in your terms. It is so difficult to translate these things from my experience into yours. The limits of your language are profound impediments when it comes to expressing the depth of not only knowing these things but experiencing them.

You are capable of experiencing them to some degree. In fact, this is how vibration is raised. You keep pushing to experience everything more deeply, recognizing that you are the creator and the created. By experiencing, you are generating emotion. Emotions are, as we have heard you say many times to your patients, your internal guidance system. The emotions literally are the indicator of how aligned you are with your Core Consciousness. When you have a pleasant emotion, you are aligned well and the energy that surges through you is unimpeded and flows smoothly. When you have an unpleasant emotion, you are being incongruent with your Core Consciousness in some part of your life. You are out of alignment with yourself, and the energy gets blocked. This unpleasant emotion has a function. It alerts you to your negative energy disrupting thoughts.

You can change the way you think. And that is imperative if you are going to learn. Once you fully understand that you are creating everything simply by the way you think of things, you realize you can either create happiness or you can create misery. Thoughts are constantly running. Have you ever tried to silence that "monkey mind" that all of you have running? It can't be done. If someone actually succeeded in doing it, their reality would collapse completely, because that internal dialogue is what keeps the structure of your reality intact. And without that structure, you as you know yourself would cease to exist.

The internal dialogue is essential, then. But letting it run unconsciously brings most individuals a lot of grief. As humans, you create your own reality with your thoughts, which arise from a core set of beliefs you formed as a young child. So, whatever you were told about the world, yourself, and others will be the foundation of your beliefs. Who you believe you are in this world is at this core. Therefore, if you are not happy, if you don't have what you want, if you are suffering you can either allow your automatic thoughts to continue to attract the reality you are manifesting that you don't want, or you can consciously focus your thoughts on what you want for yourself.

I hear you thinking. I know that skepticism. You believe deeply that it really isn't possible to change things quickly, that it isn't possible to change things entirely. That very core belief prevents it from happening. You have heard about the miracles that have happened across all cultures and over time. How do you think they happened? Wizardry? Well, sort of. If you call consciously manifesting, which is manipulating reality purposefully, Wizardry, then yes. You see, you all are doing that all the time. You just haven't been aware of it. So, you complain and cry about the injustice of the world, and you end up creating more of that for yourself.

If you want to be wealthy, dream it, allow yourself to feel it. Then you will attract it. If you want anything, it is the same principle. Focus on how it feels to have what you want, how it looks, how it smells, what it sounds like. All of it. Bask in the feeling of having it. Then it will manifest. Sometimes it happens instantly. Then the cancer is cured, the inventor changes the world, the dreamer becomes the great leader."

Journal Entry:
8-20-16

I am getting very good at joining my consciousness with that of other things and people. This morning I rode along with a very small, winged bug crawling on the ground next to me. I felt myself scooting along red rock, face down, scaling a cliff in a crack, barreling along. I had a sense of purpose, a mission. Then I pulled back and lost the bug as it blended into the gravel at my feet.

DISCOVERING THE GREAT I AM

I walked down main street in Cortez, Colorado. I came here to write. As I left the motel, I walked looking slowly at everything and enjoying the warmth and vibrant colors. Suddenly, I heard footsteps behind me and a car passed close to me by and honked. It startled me and I whipped around. There was a young black man who stepped around me apologizing. I also apologized and stated the horn had startled me. He proceeded on in front of me.

He was in his 20s, dressed in black pants and a crisp linen appearing shirt. Without even trying, I blended my consciousness with his. I felt his fear. He had also been startled by the horn and my turning and reflexively jumping at his presence. I felt him think, "What if she screams, what if someone thinks I'm trying to assault or rob her, what if she reports me because that is what she thought?" I watched him walk briskly in front of me up the road. He was so very careful, crossing the streets at only the cross walks. At one point, he paused and looked up and down the highway as if he wanted to cross to the other side. I could sense his thinking that breaking the law by crossing the road where there was no cross walk could result in something terrible. He was a young black man in America, and I experienced his baseline fear. After a pause, he continued to the next cross walk a fair distance away.

I sensed he was an intelligent man who had no history of aggression or violence, and that he was continually aware of his surroundings, always on guard, that he was keenly aware of his vulnerability that at any time a other men could, if they chose to, target him for some insignificant thing and it could be deadly. Or not. That's just the thing. It was that lack of certainty I could feel. His presence was guarded and on alert.

I walked to the city park where there was an event being set up. I stopped and asked two young women what was happening. As I did, I noticed a thin man in a dull orange jumpsuit. He was lighting a cigarette and I felt his attention upon me. One of the girls' mothers stopped to talk as well. I knew she and the man were familiar in some way, perhaps married, maybe brother and sister. They paid no attention to each other whatsoever. I decided not to continue down the side street through a neighborhood. It felt unwelcoming and I felt vulnerable.

I began to walk back to the front of the visitor center. The man followed me. I turned and saw him, and he feigned looking at something. But he kept following. I varied my path, he followed. Then I decided to confront him. I considered yelling out, "Hey, if you are following me, stop it." But I didn't. There were very few people around. I sat down on a bench and watched him with an unbreaking gaze and ready to confront him as he strolled past me within a few feet acting like he was on his way to somewhere. He rounded the building and stopped, looking back at me. We made eye contact and I sent my message, "leave me alone", with my expression, my eyes, and my energy. He left and walked around the building. But when I resumed my path back to my motel, he was there around the corner watching and waiting.

Two young men approached me. I stopped them, asked them to stand with me and explained why. They were delightful and agreed. They played in a rock band with the Christian group in the park setting up for a fund raiser. They were obviously somewhat alarmed by what I was saying about the man tracking me but stayed cool and only left when I said the man was gone and I could "make a break for it".

In retrospect, I realize that I was experiencing a clear lesson in opposites. The man who followed me was projecting an energy toward me that was malicious. I don't know what he had in mind, but it wasn't something I wanted. My gut told me what to do and I wasn't afraid, just prepared. Nothing he did appeared out of the ordinary that someone would have noticed. But he was focused on me and plotting. I felt his energy.

The young black man, on the other hand, had a good aura, although a restricted one due to his hyperawareness. He watched everything, including his own reactions and actions, gauging everything for safety.

I'm reading people all the time now. I could have told the man who followed me about his methamphetamine use. I knew he was traveling with the woman and the Christian group but was not embracing of their mission. He had been incarcerated and hooked up with the woman, who I think was his sister, because he had nowhere and nothing else to do, and being with her was safer. He had a history of incarcerations and legal problems. He was a thief and a criminal, and a predator.

The young black man, I could have told him, was educated. He was a new age kind of intellectual and was a conservationist. He was very uncomfortable and not a resident of the community. We were both experiencing an uncomfortable vulnerability.

Here, at Hovenweep, it is silent. (*Hovenweep is an ancient Freemont Native American ruin on the border of Utah and Colorado in the US.*) There is the mildest of breezes off and on, the buzz of an insect, and the silence is parted every once in a great while by the sound of a distant car. I am this scene around me, alone in the silence of this ancient desert. When I was sitting by the pool at breakfast, I saw a raven flying and I could perceive the waves of air its flapping wings created. I saw those waves rippling outward from around the bird, and as they expanded, I noticed the absolutely still air begin to move slightly, almost imperceptivity. The movement of air was so subtle that it felt like a faint delicate series of spider webs brushing my face. Then the waves passed. The bird was long out of sight.

Channeling:

"Sherry, everything affects everything else. Any change in one molecule affects multitudes of others. The effect builds until there is a critical mass of consciousness which moves things. People begin to demand that their representatives really represent them, that the institutions that one supports begin to support them, that those making decisions be transparent in their motives and practices. As the bird stirred the air with its wings, you Sherry, and you of like vibration, are stirring things with your ideas and emotions. Change is inevitable. Joining together in spirit is essential and leads to the joining of efforts to move change and create something new.

Women must begin to allow themselves to take the lead now. The feminine has long been suppressed so that the masculine could manifest, and your species could explore that alternative. It was in no way mandatory but was a choice of human consciousness. Now it is time for feminine expression. Neither the masculine nor the feminine are better than each other; nor are they opposites. They are merely complimentary energies that express compatible but different characteristics.

It is time for the women of this world to dream a new reality, one that expresses the characteristics of feminine energy. The earth needs it to save humanity from being destroyed, the people need it to transform from waring and selfishness to the realization that are all one consciousness being expressed in various ways. As your Christ is reported to have said, loving others as oneself is truly the same as loving one's self. He meant just that in a literal sense. Your neighbor IS you. Extend that to all creation. It is you, all you.

Take care of your creation, from the earth to your own body. Glory in consciously expressing that which is within you. That is true creativity and the core of being an artist.

We sense that people are very afraid right now. You are afraid. Don't listen to the fear. It can't even tell you what you are afraid of, can it? It will evaporate as you take a few meager steps and just focus on guiding others. Only those who are ready and who want to advance will hear you. Don't worry. Some will scoff and turn to their TV sets and keep getting up every day believing that the only thing before them is the job, the bills, the social climbing, the kids, the stress of being enough and doing enough in their own eyes as well as in others'. But those who hear will join together in consciousness and a group will form, and if the intension is to bring as many individuals as you can to this knowing, raising individual and mass vibrations, then it will be.

Fear is your worst enemy. It, like any and every other emotion, generates more of itself. Manage your focus, dream your dream constantly, keep putting one foot in front of the other. You are capable of conscious manifestation now. You have chosen to show others who have not learned this yet to learn it, just like you used your books to show you the mysteries, the possibilities, and introduced you to some of the greatest teachers to have been manifested on earth.

You want to use Ayahuasca. Do it. It is a mentor, an ally that can help you silence your ego long enough to glide through the veil to other possibilities of manifestation. You are strong enough. You won't get lost or not return. How do I know this? Because it is precisely that you have such a strong ego that you hesitate at the threshold and pull back that shows you are capable of it. Only one with a strong ego who can call consciousness back to the body when the body needs it should try to travel the dimensions open to it.

So, take heart. You can do this. Go create what you want. How can you teach it without doing it? Like consciousness and manifestation, they are the same thing."

8-21-16

Channeling:

"Sherry, you asked consciousness for some lessons. Today you were provided with one that clearly defined for you how you can use your consciousness in a "real world" useful way. These things are gifts. They are for everyone. Like anyone else who expands their consciousness and explores their capabilities, you wonder if what you are experiencing is real, if it is legitimate. Your fear that the communication between us is not "real" is absurd.

What is reality? It is whatever you create, project into the field of possibilities, and then observe as separate from yourself. You are wired to do this. You and all your species create thought forms which you manifest for your observation and experience. You grow and expand as you do. And when you do, all Consciousness expands as well.

The idea of a God existing outside you, apart from you, is a left over from the early days of your current series of manifestations on this planet. 300,000 years ago humans came to this planet, tinkered with the DNA of a hominid by mixing it with their own, and created you, hybrids with all of the potential of those beings, but uniquely suited to this level of vibration.

Those beings were lords over their creation. They were so advanced and could do so many unexplainable things that their creations regarded them as Gods. They were/are just as human as you are, but almost immortal. That is something that they didn't give to you. It has been reserved for later. Once your species has advanced to where you can join the galactic community as peers, it will become an option for you.

You can also see the remnants of their jealousies, their egos, their loyalties, and their greed in your own institutions which are products of the evolution of the society and social roles they left with you. Your wars, your nationalism, blind loyalties to your leaders, your tribalism, your religions, your inclination to think of people unlike yourself as "less than" all stem from those "Gods" and their own arguments with each other, often with you as pawns in their game of superiority. It is no coincidence that Europe and Asia, where the wealthy among them settled, was structured with lords presiding over areas of land and people whom they ruled and possessed. The original lords had what appeared to be powers, weapons, and abilities that your early relatives could only understand within the context of either magic or abilities of Gods. And if you think about it, a large number of you still believe this.

Those lords became divine Gods and, as they reproduced among themselves and with their hybrid race, they passed the rule and accompanying wealth from generation to generation. Remember, both the ruling class (as they became) and those whom they ruled believed the rulers were God's representatives and chosen rulers on earth.

The details of those beliefs have changed a bit, but the essence has not. And you are constantly arguing among yourselves about who is superior, who is the privileged group. "Our God is greater than yours. We are the chosen, the blessed, the entitled." Did it ever occur to you that the early "creators" are still here with you? That you are still just pawns in their games? That they are still exploiting your labor, your loyalty, you? They love it when you fight. They lay their bets on who will win; they enjoy the sport. They gather earth's resources for their own use through you. Some of them are fond of you. Many of them are not. Some are fascinated by the free will zone experiment that you are creating. Some have no fondness for you and would just as soon exploit you or see your demise.

There is a contract in place, an agreement. You can use your free will to the extent that they permit. They want to see what you will do with this. And it isn't the first time. Your species has risen and fallen a multitude of times before. What will you choose this time? Remember, you are in multiple universes, in many different experiments. And in many of those probabilities we are having this conversation or one of its probable alternatives. So, of course, I am speaking to the YOU manifesting in many dimensions reading this page. The contract states they cannot intervene in the process that you are going through, unless the counsel in charge agrees. The counsel is composed of leaders from the galactic community of which your planet is a part.

Keep in mind, they all have their own investment in you, their own interests. Like your species, they are unique in their own species-ness. After the galactic war over the earth and its resources, the contract was developed. Think it of something like your Geneva Convention which is a set of rules agreed upon by the nations that won the Second World War and which also keeps the influence of the defeated countries in check. It is an agreement, but not all of the species involved in it are there for the same reason or comply with it scrupulously. It's a situation in process that is evolving much like your own political situations. No one really knows what the outcomes will be or when things will happen. But there are patterns in general.

You are confronted, at this time, with a world that is traveling through its revolution around the galaxy and is heading into a time of physical transition related to that. Your earth is changing; have you noticed? More precisely, climate change is just one of the manifestations of your galactic cycle. Many species have permanently left the planet. Others are becoming more dominant. It's not bad or good, because there is no celestial distinction, but could be very unpleasant for humanity.

The second factor is that your own evolution (and this is a spiritual evolution that manifests in the physical) is at a transitional point. Many of you are at the forefront of a very rapid evolution of consciousness. The vibration of everyone and everything is increasing due to the rise of vibration that many of you are manifesting. You are leading the way for the flood gates to open to many of you ascending in vibration significantly. Many of you will choose to leave this vibrational frequency completely, having mastered manifestation within it. Some of you love this process, some tolerate it. We all have our preferences.

For many of us at our level of vibration, we have enjoyed manifesting within your vibrational frequency. The medium produced by it is quite enjoyable. Now, I must say I had many painful and unpleasant experiences when I was manifesting alongside you. But at my level, one can see how those are the very experiences that propel an individual to take a "leap of faith". It is there that an individual can unconsciously, or even consciously if one is more evolved, participate in the manifestation of consciousness, create deliberately, and realize on an experiential level that they are God, they are everyone and everything. We are all one consciousness. That is the meaning of you, of this level of vibration. To discover your own divinity and to assume the identity of the creator that you are.

You create it all. You are wired in your very DNA to do that. Even though you don't know how you do it, even though you don't know how to control it, even though you have not mastered creating consciously, you are doing it. You create your own reality. You create yourselves. You create your world, your experience. Once you accept final responsibility you can learn to use it to your benefit and enjoyment.

I have heard some say, "I didn't create the misery I am experiencing, the pain and suffering." Oh yes you did. You just aren't aware of it. You had your reasons. The big reason is that you are pushed closer to the knowing of who you really are by these experiences. If you didn't have them, you would never come to that realization, never learn to use it, never create consciously. You would hide behind your amnesia indefinitely and pretend things just happen, you are simply experiencing being down on your luck, you were randomly hit with misfortune. Look deeper into your own consciousness. Look into your resistance and move it aside. It will lead the way to enlightenment. It is within you, each of you, not outside you where you imagine it to be. Go within. Everything is there."

Journal Entry:
8-27-16

What has changed for me since discovering that my Story was a fiction is that I now know I have created everything in my life in a literal sense.

Everything is just a metaphor for something more, which is a metaphor for something even more, and so on. Each step, each act, each decision was designed by me to move me into more complete alignment with the flow of consciousness, the fragment of the consciousness I call myself. I have begun to really see how I made my choices, even the ones that led to pain and unhappiness. I take complete responsibility for everything in my life, whether I understand the big picture behind the surface situations or not.

It is that act that has again taken me into a deeper place in consciousness. Just when I am at a pivotal point that I am beginning to incorporate into my manifesting more fully, another level of understanding opens up even more profound. Unfortunately, the translation of it into a readable explanation isn't fully possible. So much on an experiential level is lost in translation. But that stretching for more understanding deepens awareness, and higher vibrational energy is what causes the growth.

Experiencing those things that are unbelievably painful, we psychologically move ourselves closer to self, closer to the alignment where energy flows and creativity is unrestrained. And that's the reason we choose it. Rather, that is the reason we interpret our manifestations in such an uncomfortable and painful way. It moves us.

Would anyone say I chose cancer because I wanted to go through radiation, surgeries, and chemotherapy, plus an ovarian hysterectomy because I was now a high risk for ovarian cancer? No. I didn't choose it on this level of vibration and manifestation. I chose it from a higher perspective where the self knew I was the creator. I knew I needed something radical to move me into alignment because I had resisted the lessons I had given myself prior to that and still hadn't shifted far enough.

I chose to not die.

It worked. The cancer experience, along with experiencing the guilt and witnessing the pain in the lives of my children, provoked movement that changed the direction of my life. My granddaughter chose to come to this vibration and to die before karma and the seduction of this medium took over. She had a purpose. I suspect it was to either finish something for herself or to help those who were closest to her to experience the pain that would help shift them in their own stories and in the manifestation of their own realities. Possibly both. Her parents and sister also chose this experience for their own reasons and growth. No one wants to suffer, but history is replete with those talking about what their suffering has meant to them and what they have learned.

Such is also the meaning behind suffering guilt. Feeling guilty is meant to move the individual through the suffering to alignment with their higher self. Suffering provokes us to move in a different direction using our intention. Those who learn find meaning in their suffering and become more conscious creators of their reality, which influences the reality of the whole of consciousness. Those who don't learn will continue to have increased and repeated suffering until they do.

I see more clearly now how important it is to take complete responsibility for everything in one's life. Although it doesn't make sense to our logical minds and is counter intuitive, it frees the ego to let go of its denial and resistance so that it doesn't interfere with consciousness as it creates. It allows the ego to relax and to let go of control. It also allows it to release its guilt about its flawed choices and frees it to realize it doesn't have to be perfect.

The blessed effect is that consciousness finds itself freer to create. Suddenly, the individual can become consciously aware of creating what it imagines and dreams. At that point the ego, which is feeling smaller and less overburdened, steps up and takes over the dreaming process. We begin to allow ourselves to really dream about the life we want, the world we want, the love we want. We feel it all flow through our energy body, the one that gives manifestation to the physical one. We know on a more complete level that they are the same thing, that energy moves out of the center of its body consciousness, slows and then manifests as the solid thing we both perceive and create from the energy of the consciousness deeper within ourselves.

Like the forming of a cloud as it creates itself from the inside out from condensing vapor, our physical bodies are the condensing of energy, slowing its vibration down dramatically. The human perceives only a tiny portion of the energy, just that part that the senses will perceive. But the body energy extends beyond what we can perceive in all directions, both at a slower vibrations and faster ones.

It is simply more than the computer/receivers we call brains can perceive, much less conceive of. I used to think I had to understand it all; and believe me, I still want to. But I have discovered that isn't necessary to become a conscious creator of reality. Most of it is accomplished well beyond our perceptions. But like the energy that flows from source through us to manifest at every moment and level of vibration, so does consciousness.

Consciousness and its energetic manifestation are the same thing. And so, at this level of manifestation, it is enough to know how to create within this physical medium. One doesn't have to know how it works, just that it works. There are some very concrete steps one can take to achieve conscious manifestation. And, of course, practice makes perfect.

I have reviewed my own process through the rereading of my journals and the writing of this book. It didn't go the way I expected at the outset of this book at all. But it did yield the most magnificent insights and help me to identify how I came to conscious manifestation.

I never expected to start "channeling". It happens when I send out a question to higher consciousness and it is just that spontaneous. If I don't write it down I lose the content. I'm always amazed when I reread what I have channeled, amazed at what I'm being told and amazed that it is so easy and happening at all.

Journal Entry: Channeling
8-28-16

"Sherry, you have been asking lately for more of an explanation of UFOs and aliens. Simply put, it is as Carl Sagan said when he was with you. He stated that if you were the only expression of life in the universe it would be a "terrible of space". It is very innocent of your species to believe they are the only ones. Remember when you insisted that the earth was flat? Galileo was

risking his life with his gravity theory and Copernicus was as well by saying the earth revolves around the sun. Believing that you are the only "advanced" life (and I say the word "advanced" tongue in cheek) is no different.

There is more life and more variety of life that you can possibly imagine. Literally, now. And if you consider all of the endless probabilities of you and your world in this very moment as well, it boggles the mind very quickly.

Life is always manifested in the medium native to its vibration. Therefore, life or objects coming from other planets may be very similar to you because the vibration of the universe you perceive is basically fourth dimensional. Now I am speaking of the part that you can perceive in some way. Because, if you remember, manifestation of consciousness MUST HAPPEN. All manifestation is consciousness which vibrates along a continuum that varies in frequency and intensity. What, in your description, you could consider one fragment of consciousness vibrates through multiple dimensions and is manifested in each one using the medium of the dimension.

It is safe to say that in other dimensions your consciousness "appears" within the creative medium of that frequency as very different from the manifestation you consider to be you. It is also safe to say that any other manifestation of consciousness entering your vibration would appear manifested from the medium of Fourth Dimensional reality. As that consciousness continues through other dimensions, it takes on the "appearance/behavior" of the medium at that level.

Many of the fractals of consciousness that travel to your level of vibration are not coming from huge distances. Rather, there is no here or there. They are not going anywhere. They are matching your vibration and spontaneously will manifest, and you will perceive that manifestation with your sight, sound, and touch. You will take that raw data and will fit into your preconceived beliefs of what reality is, discard or forget data that doesn't fit, and continue on your merry way believing that you are perceiving objective reality. You are not. You are perceiving the manifestation of your beliefs and expectations, individually and in mass. You cannot know the reality of any entity visiting your level of vibration if you cannot match their vibration. And if you do, you will appear to them as something within their own mass created reality using the medium of that vibration. Get it? Everything is real. Nothing is real.

Your species is one of limitless forms of life. It is no more valid than any other and no less valid than any other. When you destroy the manifestation of consciousness around you (your world), you are destroying yourself. When you destroy life, you destroy yourself. Look at your wars. It's impossible for you to tell who is on what side and what is happening anymore. Pay attention. What is keeping the conflicts going? Who stands to benefit from those conflicts and the destruction of ancient artifacts and entire societies? Just as the answers you seek concerning consciousness can be found by going deeper into it, the answers for these questions lies within your reach if you dare to go deeper. The irony is that the deeper individuals go into it to find the answers, the more chaotic and complex the answers become. Same with consciousness, unless one is willing to give up paradigms of belief and allow new possibilities.

As with everything else, the process is one of fractals as well. The deeper one explores, the more there is to explore. Watch for repeating patterns. Keep in mind that "as above, so below" is literal whether speaking about physical manifestation, social manifestation, or consciousness. One will find the same thing at both smaller and larger. (I'm beginning to feel very limited by having to communicate in this way. The translation is a meager interpretation of the message. Want a chuckle? It's the same on this end. What we get from you after interpretation and translation sometimes doesn't make any sense to us at all.)"

9-5-16:

Channeling:

"Sherry, as you were reading some channeled information today from another fragment of consciousness, you suddenly asked (again) why you need to expose this part of yourself to the scrutiny that will inevitably come from publishing your experiences and what you have learned. The answer is that you asked for this. You sent the message that you want to help bring

the new world into being, to help yourself, to help others. You have correctly identified that you chose to incarnate this time for this reason. You wanted to share in the experience and manifestation of the great shift in consciousness that is happening right now. Consciousness is accelerating at an astonishing speed. Your desire to BE there, and to be as fully conscious as possible is why you are incarnate. So, BE there.

You asked to be on the front lines. You are delighted to be one of the frontrunners in this endeavor. But your ego is like any other ego. It is afraid of annihilation. This is a protective measure of the ego, and it is an appropriate one. Remember, we have stated before that an individual with a fragile ego can indeed be annihilated when it attempts to venture into the structure-less-ness of consciousness. Such an individual should never purposely induce a radical exploration of consciousness, such as is possible, because they may not return to this level of manifestation.

This level of manifestation was chosen by you who are incarnated within this dimension right now so that you could be part of the shift happening which will have a ripple effect throughout the physical universe and nonphysical one as well. You who are manifesting in this dimension wanted to explore it, influence it, and create within it. It is not appropriate to try to flee this level of vibration, then, because you have chosen it for yourself. You knew your specific role in the manifestation of this reality and most of you wanted it very much. Specifically, you Sherry, wanted to manifest here now.

Those of you who realize there is much more to experience are welcome to expand your energy and vibrate at a different frequency, within the constraints of the medium of course, into nearby frequencies/realities. As you have discovered, this is how one raises their personal vibration and expands. And it benefits all of consciousness, not just the portion you picture encased within your physical manifestation.

Sherry, you have been called like many others. You have expressed the desire to be part of this manifestation yourself, which is imperative. Nothing in your experience, NOTHING, is manifested without your agreement.

We are you, you are us. There are no divisions. And as we have stated before, the nature of consciousness is to create itself. It combines, shifts, and is no more a discrete and separate package than an ocean of water is separated by its individual molecules and atoms. On some level, the ego knows this and it feels threatened with annihilation. All manifestations of consciousness are forever. Any can be called forth at any time, and consciousness does this all the time. The ego is never destroyed.

Some incarnations have very pleasant and rewarding situations within them. Consciousness will sometimes select to revisit that fragment, that specific fractal of itself, to re-experience itself within that frequency. And of course, it is much bigger than this. All possibilities are being created at once, all variations of possibilities, each giving rise to new possibilities. We are speaking now in very simple terms in order that we can convey some truths about "reality" in a way that can be understood.

We are aware of your feelings of insecurity in exposing yourself by tapping into our vibration and in writing this book. Everyone feels the same, because of the common agreement that this is impossible. That it is not "real". It is given names that invalidate the experience, such as psychosis and delusion. At the very least, you will be and are often regarded by others as strange, odd. Can you learn to live with that?

It is necessary to model for others this capability that all humans have inherited as a birthright. Everyone will eventually find that they have this capability as their own fractal of vibration rises. And this is the reason you have been asked, and you have agreed to write this book. It is by individuals connecting with this capability of consciousness, showing others how to do it, that all will come to realize anyone can tap into this level of creativity and knowledge as well. Our goal at this level of vibration, one of many, is to help people realize that putting anyone or anything, whether it be a medium or a religious icon, between themselves and the source of all that is, is a paradigm within the old way of thinking. Everyone is capable of connecting with source, the consciousness of the larger self. That is how the new world will be formed, by conscious individuals deliberately creating a better world, one with a higher vibration.

You questioned again what to call us. You were reading how "so and so" is channeling "so and so" and said to us, "Why would I have anything more to reveal that hasn't been revealed by others before?" It is precisely because you are channeling information in agreement with those others who are doing the same thing. You MUST write it down and disseminate it so others will be validated, so that the knowledge becomes more mainstream and acceptable, and so that others know that everyone has the capability of tapping into this expansion of consciousness that can be so very gratifying. This is occurring. Every wonder why organized religion appears to be receding worldwide? More and more, people are recognizing that they are the best channel for spirit, that they are their own spiritual authority.

We have suggested before that you refer to us, if you must refer to us as something, as S +. Or if you prefer, refer to us as THE S'. Names are completely irrelevant, however. We simply give you and others like you a name to use to refer to us so that you can find this experience more familiar. It is a way of structuring your experience in an understandable way for you. However, it isn't necessary at all. And as individuals come to expand themselves further, letting go of old paradigms of belief about what is reality, names will become obsolete and the useless concepts that they represent will be exposed. We are all just fractals of consciousness in a gestalt of consciousness. We are all one.

There is no one voice, no one person, no one way to present this information to the populations of consciousness now manifesting within your reality. Many heard the call and many have responded to do this work so that it will be disseminated throughout your societies as effectively as possible. Your voice is as important as any other. Your specific vibration will resonate with those of like vibration. Your unique perspective which has been influenced by your interest in identifying what God is (is not), blended with your education and work in mental health, and even the hard years in nursing will present this information in a unique way. It will be both a self-help book and an instruction for therapists to use in helping their patients make desired change in their lives. It will make a difference.

You might ask why it is at all important for you and those others like you to bring this information to the mainstream. It is because your species, all species on the earth and the earth herself are going through a dramatic rise in vibration. You have been positioned in this place now to help propel yourselves through the difficulties that are coming and, especially, in order to form a new world, a more elevated one in the eternal expansion and manifestation of consciousness.

You, all incarnate beings, are poised at the precipice of unmarked territory. And you have been here before. Your religions and myths have all recognized this time as a time of either the failure of your species to advance, or the success of doing so and creating something that has never before been created. There are no maps for you. Your job, if you choose to accept it (I sensed a smirk), is to create the new. If your species chooses to resist the movement of consciousness in this direction, you will be reset, as has happened so often before, and begin again. It's an exciting time for all consciousness manifesting throughout the cosmos. But if you choose to not advance, that is your choice. Nothing is ever wasted, only experienced in a different way. Expansion is inevitable and will occur regardless of an unlimited number of resistances.

Be brave. Trust the process of expansion. You wanted to be part of it, you have wanted it your entire life. We suggest you seize this opportunity to fulfill your desires and goals. Choose what you like. You are God, God is everything, everything is You. Grow, expand, create, experience. We support you in this endeavor. Through your work, you will ascend. All of consciousness will."

Part Three

RECIPE FOR CONSCIOUS MANIFESTATION

> You have the choice. You can live the illusion of a life of duality with all its many problems or you can realize that everything is one. You are not part of a divine all powerful source, you are that divine powerful source. Once you truly understand that, you can create miracles.
> —Unknown

As I read through my journal entries while transcribing those that I felt provided a picture of my spiritual growth, I became aware that the process I had been through to learn to manifest consciously what I wanted in this life and beyond needed to be identified and spelled out to help others do the same. I was told through channeled information that I needed to do this, that it is the "mission" of my life to present this material in my own way in order to create a map for those who resonate with my process and want to follow it. All my training, formal and informal, all my experiences, personal and professional, have led me to this moment. I have been preparing for this for my entire life. Therefore, I have developed the following recipe to help clarify and define the specific steps I used to arrive at this point of my personal manifestation.

I started with the realization that the story of my life that I repeated to myself and others was a fiction based upon my core beliefs. We all have a story we believe which is formed from a handful of core beliefs that we simply accept as fact. They are embedded into our world view and we view everything in our lives through the lens of those beliefs. We observe the environment and situations around us, choose the information that fits into our preconceived beliefs, use it to fortify and validate those beliefs, and ignore what doesn't fit.

Again, we all do this. When we realize what we are doing, usually because we have become miserable, we often feel unable to change the patterns in our lives that show up over and over again in various scenarios. My core belief was that I was "a good girl", which meant that I had to live by the rules and keep everyone else happy, I had no right to define for myself what I wanted, to be my authentic self, to speak my truth. All of my other beliefs were based upon that one. And all of my lessons were meant to provoke me to determine not only what I wanted and didn't want, but to see myself as having the right to insist upon having what I wanted from my life.

I have seen a very similar belief system in people who have allowed themselves to become involved in abusive situations. We build our lives one decision at a time and end up producing for ourselves the exact lessons we need to move us into alignment with our higher selves. Those lessons are based upon a core belief which is limiting us and creating pain and despair.

This is the very reason we exist in this dimension. When we incarnate, we bring with us our entire experience from all our incarnations and other levels of existence. As I have stated before, we are all part of the same consciousness without any real divisions. Our choice to come to this earth, at this specific time, in this reality, is to create something new that will expand all of consciousness through our individual growth.

Our emotions are our internal guidance system. Emotions are neither good nor bad. They simply are there to move us into better alignment with our higher selves. When we experience something uncomfortable, we are forced to become more conscious of what we have created for ourselves and why. As we grow up we lose the open connection with All That Is Consciousness that is ours as young children. The world and what we have been taught to pay attention to takes over and we get carried away in the illusion of our belief systems.

Our emotions are designed to move us back to the flow of God consciousness, to All That Is, where we can embrace our creation. When we are not true to ourselves, we compromise a part of ourselves that is essential and that is what creates pain. Being in alignment is being an open channel for consciousness and being authentically ourselves. Discomfort and pain drive us to realign.

We are constantly creating ourselves and our realities. We do it automatically. Not only do our core beliefs about ourselves determine what we create, but they keep us operating within a narrowly defined description of reality. Information from quantum mechanics has shown that what we consider to be reality is superficial and plastic. We perceive only a tiny fraction of the data through our senses which is before us. And to make it even more mysterious, the data before us is a faithful description of our beliefs using the energy of this dimension and projected like a hologram into our perceptive field. It is only as "real" as our beliefs are. And they are invariably fiction. Many are self-defeating.

When we are born and until about the age of seven we are taught what is "real". We are taught what to believe about everything. It becomes the core of who we define ourselves to be and what we define as our reality. We are all in basic agreement about reality because it is how our attention has been trained and it shapes all that we perceive. What we focus on is what we invariably create.

I know of someone who was able to see entities her entire life that most of us cannot perceive. She would be talking to someone and begin to stare above their shoulder. Sometimes she would speak to what her parents assumed was an imaginary friend. She was alright with this ability, until she was about 8 or 9 when she realized that other people couldn't see or hear the things she did. Then she became terrified. She thought something was wrong with her, that she was crazy, that an evil entity was threatening her and she kept her ability to herself for a long time, until she could keep quiet no longer.

She was "treated" by professionals. As a young adult, she no longer perceives these entities. Nor is she willing to talk about them. My guess is she either lost the ability to perceive them when she realized she wasn't supposed to see them, or she has figured out that it is probably in her best interest to not talk about them.

Many years back there was a woman who became Miss America. She talked about how she was the shining star of her family: the straight A student, cheerleader, popular teen who was the pride and joy of her parents. She went to college, won the Miss America pageant, then met a man and was planning to marry when she collapsed and fell apart. She suddenly remembered having a daytime identity and a nighttime identity. She recalled that her father had sexually abused her every night for years.

One might ask how this is possible, to forget such a thing that occurred night after night year after year and not be able to remember it. But it happens. If one doesn't have the paradigm of beliefs in which the experience can be stored, it simply gets stored in a remote corner of memory where the information is not easily accessed, or it is ignored. For us to remember and incorporate our experiences, we must have a structure in which to store incongruent memories and pathways to access them. She grew up being told she was one thing and simply didn't have the belief structure to accommodate the part of her experience that was entirely incongruent with her beliefs. Maybe she told her mother when it happened and her mother, also unable to incorporate that information, dismissed it in some way. Perhaps her mother told her child she was lying and to never mention it again. In any case, the experience of her nights went invalidated and lost their reality. I have this dynamic in my professional practice many times.

This is an extreme example, but a real one. The same process occurs with all of us moment by moment. We select what fits with our beliefs and forget or dismiss the rest. Denial is a powerful coping mechanism which is very useful in helping us survive. But it can lead to limiting ourselves, as any coping mechanism can.

I bring this up because the first step in moving beyond our current state is to recognize that our story is just a fiction based upon our core beliefs and formed around our interpretations of our experiences. It is imperative that we recognize this and that we take complete responsibility for every aspect of our lives if we are to change anything. We must know our story, know that it is a story of our own making, and accept that we have created it all if we are to be able to write a new one. One that is more authentic, one we want, that we deliberately choose. Although it feels counterintuitive, this reality is more real than what we have come to accept as real.

I don't know of anyone who wouldn't like to make their dreams come true, who wouldn't change something in the flow of their lives. So often we believe that what happens to us is random, or that it is chosen by a deity apart from us, or that things just happen and we are born into circumstances that are dire, or that others are responsible for our uncomfortable and painful experiences. We pray, appeal for help, blame, and often give into fear and despair. We refuse to be responsible for our lives because our ego says, "I wouldn't choose this for myself".

I will not get into a discussion about whether we create and choose everything for ourselves. There will always be an argument about that, usually based in resistance. However, I do know what works and taking responsibility for everything in our lives is necessary if we are to learn to manifest what we want consciously. The very simple act of taking responsibility opens the individual to being able to follow specific steps to create what they want. Otherwise, we take refuge in denying responsibility. We will go so far as to agree that we are complicit but refuse to accept we are the designers of our experience…start to finish.

In Alcoholics Anonymous there is a saying, "Let go and let God." The first step is to admit powerlessness over our lives. This may seem like a contradiction with my assertion that one must take full responsibility, but it isn't. It is not the identity in this dimension, the ego, that decides the setting of one's birth and life. The ego doesn't decide to make the body sick (usually) or to bring about horrible accidents and mishaps. It is your higher self, the portion of your immediate fractal of consciousness that is just beyond ordinary self-awareness that makes these determinations. And those choices are based upon the overall goal: realigning ordinary consciousness with All That IS and creating consciously. Conscious manifestation is the birth right of every individual born to this earth.

Others down through the ages have identified this as the starting point as well. It is perhaps presented differently by different people in various cultures, but the mechanism and intension are the same. Once one takes responsibility for everything in their life, they can then stop blaming themselves and others, stop complaining, stop distracting themselves with their discomfort and get down to the business of creating what they want. The ego is then off the hook because it has been unconsciously participating in manifestation without any control. It has been blamed and beaten up in most of us. It has been focusing our manifestation power on the things we attract but don't want. Once we take personal responsibility, the ego becomes a great asset. It can dream our lives. It can focus our intention on what we want to manifest. It can muster our will power. Within its limitations, it can create consciously. Then it can simply leave it up to the part of consciousness that does the actual work of manifestation to create everything else.

The reason our higher selves choose pain, suffering, and discomfort is that, in order to manifest consciously, we must know precisely what it is that we don't want, and we must be miserable enough to let go of. Suffering provokes the ego to recognize what it cannot control, allowing it to function unimpeded. There is no better way to be motivated to do something than to be compelled to make changes so that we are not miserable.

Think about it. If you are comfortable and satisfied, do you want to change anything? Not usually. You may still have things you would like to accomplish, but to make significant changes in one's life one usually must be compelled to do so...until we learn to create consciously. And these changes that I am suggesting are so core to who we think we are that it requires effort.

It begins by identifying the core beliefs we hold, the ones we accept as reality and never question. We apply those core beliefs to ourselves and everyone else, accepting them as truth when they are only beliefs we formed when we were small children and infants. They are downloaded to us by the people and events closest to us. They define who we are, what the world is about, and who we are within it. They become the lens through which we perceive the everything in our lives and how we attribute causality.

So, having laid the groundwork for change, here is how to do it. I base this on my own experience and with what I have learned working as a psychotherapist with children and families. I have examined my own story and documented my psychological and psychic movement since before the discovery that my story is a fiction based upon core beliefs. I will attempt to break down the process I went through and to present it in such a way that others can follow a similar path and, hopefully, become the conscious manifest-masters of their lives.

A brief description of how this works is probably needed. Remember the dysfunctional family based upon a closed system that holds the homeostasis of the family? Our minds function the same way. As we grow, we incorporate data along with the interpretation of that data. We develop a core belief and the other deep beliefs that support it. We have a running dialogue that reinforces it which becomes the fabric of our lives. Our thoughts, our emotions, and our behaviors are linked to that core belief and reinforced by the running dialogue in our minds. It is only when we interrupt this closed system that we can make any real change. Our specific cognitive loop, that ongoing retelling of our story, becomes our reality and the basis of every judgement, interpretation, and experience in our lives. Don't like something in your life, experiencing illness and physical symptoms, feel inadequate or depressed? Change the core belief and you change everything.

Years ago, as I was looking for answers. I began to read self-help books and books on spirituality and metaphysics. As I am one of those people who likes scientific explanations, I began to branch out into reading about Quantum Physics. I began to understand that science and spirituality are different explanations of the same thing. Neither of them is as exclusive as we have become conditioned to believe. Both explore creative possibilities and attempt to explain everything from who we are to what is our purpose. Quantum physics, also known as quantum mechanics, approaches these questions from the basis of science. Spirituality and metaphysics attempt the same thing through an exploration of consciousness.

Remember how the very act of observing the light wave freezes it into a particle of matter? Waves are energy which become particles, the energy stuff of matter. There are some notable scientific experiments that prove this. It is no longer just a theory.

The Double Slit Experiment was first performed by Thomas Young in 1801, before quantum mechanics was theorized. It has been replicated and expanded upon since that time. The basic experiment is conducted by a light source illuminating a plate pierced by two parallel slits, and the light passing through the slits is observed on a screen on the other side in the interference pattern it produces on the screen. Light manifests as both a wave and a particle. Therefore, light has two natures, wave patterns that are like ripples of water that cross each other, and particle like qualities that carry energy in discrete bundles that we have named photons. This experiment demonstrates that light behaves in both ways depending upon expectation and observation by an observer.

We project out what we believe, and that expectation is materialized into matter and form by using the building blocks of conscious energy that permeate everything. How that happens, we don't know. But it happens. Everything we see, everything we experience is a hologram that we project outward into our experience. We have forgotten that we are the creators of everything, and we get lost in the projection. We forget we are fiction writers and come to believe that our subjective experience is objective reality.

Remember the experiments conducted by Masaro Emoto? As mentioned earlier in the book, he did experiments with water crystals and rice, among other things. Again, what he found was that it was the intention of the observer that determined whether the polluted water formed a beautiful crystal when frozen or a mutated, ugly one. It was the expectation of the observer that determined whether the rice stayed fresh and eatable or decayed into a nasty smelling mush. External circumstances, such as the temperature in the rice experiment were irrelevant. The rice that was expected to decay because the observers were saying hateful things to it did; and the rice that had observers saying loving things to it didn't. Not because of the language of what was said or how it was said, but because of the intention and emotion of the person who said it.

Consciousness is ever present, and it must manifest; and energy is the medium of manifestation. One does not exist separate from the other.

As individuals, we gaze out through our senses upon a field of waves of energy flowing through, around, and between everything. Our expectation and focus form that frozen energy into matter. This is an unconscious process. It happens whether we are active or passive participants. Whatever we focus on, we create. The act of observation, expectation, and focus creates the manifestation.

It is precisely what we focus on, whether we are aware of doing it or not, that we will manifest for ourselves. Our constant internal dialogue not only keeps the focus on what we believe, but it keeps that belief fortified. It judges and criticizes based upon the core belief. This is a self-perpetuating system. What we fear is what we will manifest for ourselves to experience. And what we want once we have changed a dysfunctional core belief can also become what we manifest.

It all begins and ends with belief. Our core beliefs.

The wonder and the beauty is that as fractals of consciousness, we contain the ALL and we are influencing all parts of the ALL. As we become more conscious of ourselves as the creator, we are more able to create what we want. If we create love and peace within ourselves and our lives, those will be projected into form and experience. A critical mass of people with similar frequencies can create change on a large scale. That is how we will shape the new world.

We are faced with a decaying world that needs visionaries and light workers to build something new. It starts with each of us individually and flows outward like the ripples in a pond, influencing the next story of humanity. It is why we are here. It is what we have chosen, and the very fact that you are reading this means you are one of us, one who is increasing in vibration and learning to manifest consciously.

It's time to begin. It's time to stop being a passive creator and to become a deliberate one, consciously moving the evolution of humankind to higher levels of consciousness and manifestation. It is what we are designed to do.

> "The primary cause of unhappiness is never the situation but your thoughts about the situation, which is always neutral..."
> Eckhart Tolle, Aug 31, 2015
> www.goodreads.com

> "That's why you're here! You don't have to analyze this current storm to deal with it. All you have to do is stand where you are and keep the light going. That's why you came to this planet this time, and that's why you're here. Spirit promises you that you have enough light and that your lighthouse will not be destroyed, for it was built for the storm. In fact, it was built for exactly this storm."
> —Live Channelling - New York, NY
> From Lee Carroll
> 2006

THE ESSENTIAL ELEMENT OF MANIFESTATION

The foundational ingredient of manifestation is mindfulness. I have talked about it throughout this book but haven't focused on its imperative. As stated, one will manifest whatever they focus their attention upon. In order to manifest consciously what we want, we have to manage our focus. Letting the mind go unrestrained in its perpetual chatter holding the story together is unconscious manifestation. As consciousness, you cannot NOT manifest. But you may be manifesting your worst fears, your worst nightmare.

So how does one manage focus? By being MINDFUL. That means that all your attention is on what you are experiencing at that very moment. If you are eating, your attention is on the taste, the texture, and the smell of your food. Pleasant or not, that is what you are focused on. The same is true for every moment. If you are worrying in fear, you are projecting the things you are afraid of into your experience and into your future. If you are living with anxiety, you are attempting to control the future or an outcome. If you are living with depression, you are living in the past of your story that you frame with your negative core beliefs. You will probably always be somewhat unconsciously manifesting. But if you can change your destructive core belief and replace it with one you want, your self-talk begins to change to reflect the new belief, you will begin to feel more of what you want because of it, and your behavior will create and attract experiences based upon your new belief.

Ta-da! Your life will change. I don't mean to be flippant, but the concept is very simple although not easy. We are habituated to our beliefs. Our expectations are based upon them. It is the souls work to learn this process so that it can create a world where there is peace, abundance, and love. Staying consciously present is difficult to do in the beginning. It is a learned skill and one that takes repeated effort. So often I will have a patient say, "I tried mindfulness, but it didn't work."

It works. But the individual must practice it to make it work. One must discipline the thoughts one has to change the dialogue and structure of the story. It takes time, effort, and one will be continually tested to refine their expertise in doing it. Time after time the individual will find themselves repeating the same old story lines and must forcefully turn their thoughts in another direction. Keep in mind that the thoughts lead to the emotions one experiences. Once triggered our emotions can clue us in to the realization that we are operating from faulty beliefs again, and we can deliberately become mindful once more. One of the easiest ways to do this is to pull one's attention into the present by focusing entirely on the sensations of that moment and FEELING GRATITUDE FOR THEM. Even the ones we label "bad".

In addition to mindfulness, non-judgement is necessary for stepping outside of one's story. Judgement, by its nature, involves value systems which are part of the structure of the STORY. The goal is to rid yourself of your story so completely that new information can be assimilated into one's worldview. Judgement not only holds the original story in place, but it is also a warning. If you are judging anything or anyone, including yourself, it is an indicator that you are still operating within the framework of the story. One must deliberately suspend any judgement to be successful. This is not just a little part of the overall process. It is the foundation of change.

> Energy always follows a focused thought. Use your intention deliberately to create what you want. Use your will to direct your intention. Be deliberate. In this way, anything can be manifested.
> —Sherry Griffith

THE RECIPE FOR CONSCIOUS MANIFESTATION

STEP ONE: UNCOVER YOUR CORE BELIEF

- Identify Your Story
- Identify those people and situations that you attribute your negative feelings and experiences to.
- Identify the painful and uncomfortable emotions that accompany them. Label those emotions.
- Form your core belief into an "I AM…" statement about from the naming of that emotion. (For example: I am a victim. Or I am a failure."

The first step is to write your story down or you can record yourself telling it. It is important to be able to return to it to sift out the reasons you have attributed to your experience. Do you blame others? It's typical. But blaming God or anyone or anything keeps you from progressing.

Do you feel guilty? Do you feel victimized or unsafe? Do you feel unlucky or like life is nothing but a struggle? It is through seeing and understanding the patterns that run through your life that you can begin to identify your CORE BELIEF: the one about yourself that gives rise to all your other beliefs, your thoughts which reinforce your beliefs, your behavior which generates more of those beliefs, and your emotions arising from interpretation of events which are based upon that belief. If you change one, you change them all. The goal is to identify and change the core belief that is causing you pain.

As you write your story, make your rendition of it specific. Be sure to talk about significant people and events from your earliest memories to the present. Talk about why things happened in your life. Don't sanitize the story. Tap into the emotions that come with remembering them and name them. Emotions are the representations of what you believe about the events. They are your internal guidance system. Just tell your story like you always have.

The final act with each memory is to thank the person, animal, or event that brought the lesson to you, particularly focusing on those you feel have harmed you. Thank them (to yourself) out loud. Stating everything out loud will help you to crystalize your process in a way that becomes permanent. If you find you are unable to thank an individual or consciousness for a painful event, you can again connect with the emotion. Tapping on this emotion and breathing a specific way will resolve it. (We'll cover this later.)

Remember that you must accept responsibility for choosing everything in your life, as this will give you the ability to release your ego from returning to your story. Take responsibility for everything you have ever experienced, including the circumstances of the life you were born to. Remind yourself that YOU have approved of this lesson, you have designed it, and you have created it. Hopefully, the person or people helping you learn it are also learning through their own process. Again, this is absolutely essential to beginning this process. And when it comes to how long it takes, I always say, "It will take as long as you take. It's up to you. Just be willing and start with an open mind and taking responsibility for your experience."

Continue to go through your story repeatedly until you have clearly identified the themes and patterns of attribution that you believe have made you a victim, unimportant, hopelessly flawed, unsuccessful, unable to change anything in your life, not deserving, someone who has bad luck, etc. Shift out the beliefs that are negative. If a belief is working for you, you may not need to change it or it will simply take a less prominent place in your story as it shifts and eventually disappears. I don't want to dissuade anyone from looking at the more positive beliefs, but the bulk of work should focus on the negative ones, the ones keeping you from fully aligning with your higher consciousness. The "I AM" statement you uncover is the belief around which you have formed yourself and your reality. The one that leads to addictions, failures, conflicts, lack, scarcity, and misery.

This is rather threatening to the ego. It will protest: "I'm too tired to do this work, it's too hard, I have other things I need to do, it doesn't make sense, I don't believe it will work". Remember, this is the ego speaking and although it might be experiencing misery, it is comfortable in the homeostasis of the cognitive loop. Change feels annihilating. It says, "If I'm not ……., then what am I? If I'm not……., then I don't exist because I have been built on this core belief. If it changes, what will happen to me?"

Start to pay attention to the running dialogue in your head, that monkey mind of constant chatter we have with ourselves that talks to us about ourselves and the world. Notice when it is critical of you or others and what it says. Pay attention to how the dialogue ties into the core belief you have identified. That dialogue both reflects the core belief and reinforces it. That dialogue holds the story of your life together. The more you allow it to run in the background of your experience, the stronger your core belief becomes. Listening to what it says is also an effective way to identify or clarify the core belief. That chatter will tell you everything about your story and your core belief that has given rise to it.

Sometimes in this process an individual will find a new core belief, one that goes deeper than the previous one and is more precisely responsible for how they have structured their life. This may lead to a new "I Am"… statement. Doing this along with analyzing your story's patterns will lead to core belief identification…if you are willing to be honest with yourself. This could be the hardest part, because your resistance will be strong. The chatter will steadfastly insist that your core belief is true because the ego is feeling threatened, and fierce honesty coupled with a desire to change the circumstances of your life must be kept forcefully at the forefront. This is called setting your intention. Even if you don't know the direction that this will take you (very exciting, actually), your intention to make change by restructuring your core belief and the attendant beliefs is necessary. Intention backed by the will to push through your resistance and denial will keep you on track.

Then once the "I Am" statement has been formed, the one that has dominated your worldview and has led to the constant dialogue that reinforces that core belief, you are ready to change at the deepest level of personality. You are free to create a story you want to experience.

STEP TWO: CHANGING THE CORE BELIEF, LEAVING THE STORY BEHIND

- Make a list of everyone who you feel has hurt or offended you.
- Process each individual separately and thank them for participating in your awakening, in the lesson you have chosen for yourself. Identify what they helped you learn. You can use Tapping or Recapitulation breath work, or any other method you find that works for you to reprocess them. You will know if it has worked if the original uncomfortable emotion is changed to gratitude for the person and the lesson learned.
- Express gratitude to All That Is for your lesson and those who helped you learn it.
- Replace your core belief with one that is functional, that honors you.

Don Juan told Carlos Castaneda to eliminate his personal history. This is the same concept of non-attachment in Buddhism. Non-attachment and stepping outside of the story is what he meant. This will enable the individual to expand consciousness and explore possibilities of manifestation unfamiliar to us. He meant we must detach from everyone and everything in order to eliminate expectations and allow consciousness to manifest through us. We must allow others to create their own experience and let go of outcomes. In other words, we need to Let Go and Let God.

To leave behind our story, we must become empty. If we have no story, no history, no agenda, no expectations, and no attachments (meaning we are no longer trying to control things) we have become empty, and through our focus and intensions we can participate in creation. And we can do it consciously.

But how do we leave those old feelings of hurt, pain, resentment, fear and discomfort behind? It's one thing to say it and another thing to do it.

There are a couple of reliable ways to change a core belief. After taking personal responsibility for oneself, after realizing that one's story is a fictional script of one's own making, and after identifying the maladaptive core belief one holds, one must change that belief.

Changing the core belief is called cognitive restructuring. I provided an example of it in part one of this book. Essentially, the therapist or the individual will challenge the validity of their interpretation of things in their experience by presenting contrary evidence. They will break down the belief and challenge the truthfulness of the interpretation of the individual. This is effective, especially when the therapist is skilled at doing it and the individual is willing to change the way they attribute meaning to their experience. If one has access to therapy, good therapy, they can augment their growth with it. It's always a good idea to have a neutral third party to help us challenge our beliefs.

An effective therapist has identified their own story, their own faulty thinking, they have faced and experienced their own emotions and learned how they are manifesting them in their lives. They are already in their own process. One can still achieve the end result on their own if they are willing to find teachers through other means, such as books. The only requirement is that the person must be willing to open their mind and be fiercely honest with themselves.

Along with challenging beliefs, there are two other ways to do this that I prefer. Both can be done without the involvement of another person. The first was introduced by Don Juan Matis through Carlos in his books. He called it recapitulation, (The Eagles Gift, 1982) The other is Tapping.

Recapitulation: The restating or revisiting of something. The remembering of something, the re-experiencing of how our senses interpreted it.

After your list of people has been compiled, start with the first one. Allow yourself to remember and FEEL THE EMOTION of the original situation. Then breathing slowly, move your head from your left to your right as you exhale. After a pause, inhale slowly and deeply from the abdomen while rotating your head from your right to your left. Repeat until you no longer feel the emotion.

Proceed to the next person on your list and repeat the steps above. You may find you still have a feeling about a previously recapitulated person or event. If so, go back and redo them until all feeling about them is neutral.

Don Juan taught that on the inhale one would "pick up the filaments they left behind" and on the exhale the individual would be "ejecting filaments left in them by other luminous bodies" (other people). As you do this procedure you will be literally gathering back energetic parts of yourself that you left behind in the emotion of the painful experience. You will also be setting your boundaries on the energy that the person or situation is still taking from you, that you are leaking from your own luminous body. It's all about energy. And positive energy is required to do the work of conscious manifestation.

Tapping:

Tapping is an Emotional Facilitation Technique that has proven to be extremely helpful to those who want to bring about a momentous change within themselves which will be reflected in their lives. It's so easy and simple that most people don't take it seriously initially. I usually must demonstrate it to someone several times, and they have to wallow in their discomfort before they give it a real try. Then I later hear from them that it is working.

Tapping works by drawing the attention of the left brain to certain acupressure points along the meridians of the body, while saying out loud a mantra that is focused on self- love despite feelings about ourselves that are negative in nature. The right brain is left free to create new belief paradigms and to reprocess pain in a new way. As we do this, our story becomes less rigid, and we begin to allow progress.

There are numerous studies on the efficacy of tapping that show profound results. There are many ways of tapping, all of them effective. It is almost impossible to do it wrong. I suggest going to the internet, doing some basic research, and then developing your own mantras based upon the demonstrations that are available. All tapping should be personalized, specific in wording and feeling, and the uncomfortable emotion that accompanies the conglomeration of thoughts should be rated prior to starting the tapping exercise, and then rated after each round of tapping. You should see a decrease in the intensity of the bothersome emotion each time.

Tapping isn't meant to eliminate what one would consider a "bad" emotion. It reforms and allows reinterpretation, storing it in the past where it originated and where it belongs. In this way, one can dump a damaging core belief about oneself leaving a space in the cognitive loop where new information can get in and replace the old. When the original core belief is dismantled, one will find a freedom and lightness that they had not previously experienced.

Tapping Step One:

Start by holding, feeling, and naming the emotion of a past situation related to your self-destructive core belief in your mind and body. Feel it. Then rate its intensity on a scale from 1 to 10 with 10 being the highest intensity of the emotion. (Refer to the Tapping diagram.)

TAPPING DIAGRAM

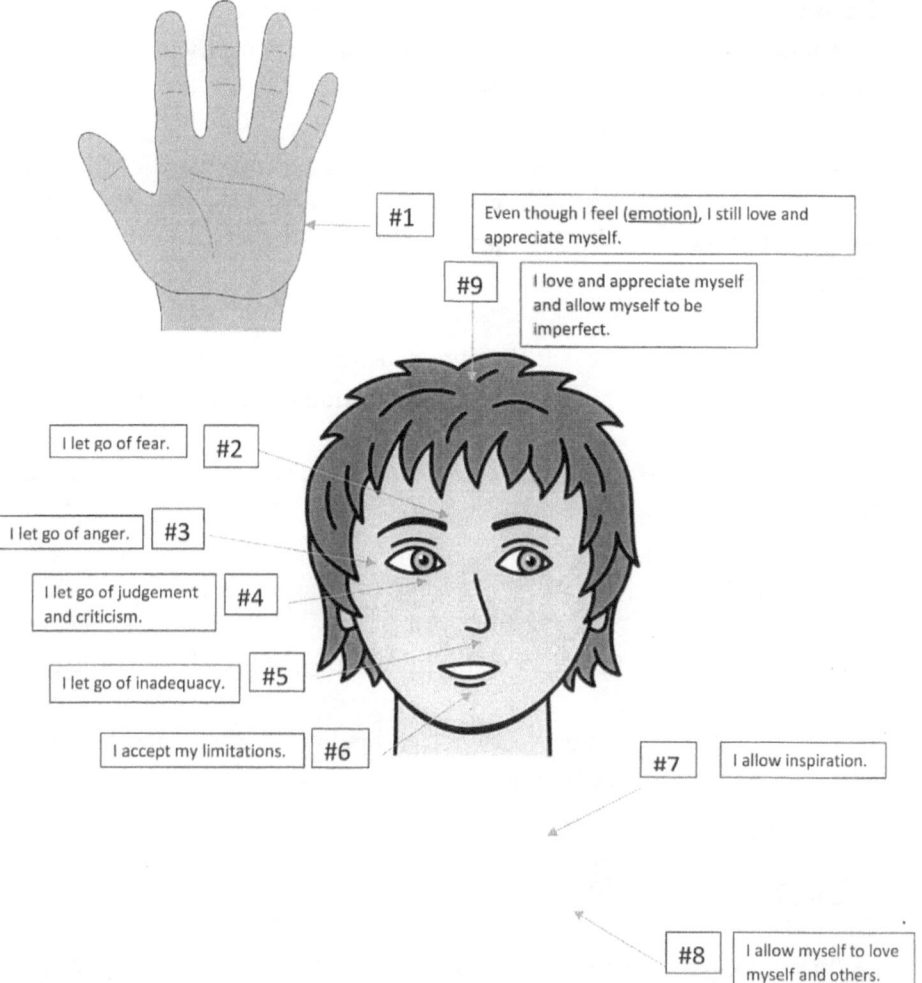

Start tapping with your first two fingers of your dominant hand the area on the side of Tapping Step Two:

Start with your dominant hand and tap your other hand as in the diagram. Tap repeatedly and firmly and say step one of your mantra. This is a sort of grounding statement that ties the whole sequence together. State, "Even though I feel..., I still love and appreciate myself."

Move to #2 over the eye on the dominant hand side, and with the same two fingers tap repeatedly and firmly the bony part of the eye socket near the inner part of the eyebrow. Say the second part of your mantra, such as, "I let go of anger".

Proceed to #3 on the bone at the outer side of the same eye. Tap and say your third mantra, such as, "I let go of perfection in myself and others".

Proceed to #4 on the bone under the same eye and state the fourth mantra. "I let go of pain."

Then to the 5th (on the mustache), "I let go of disappointment".

6th (under the bottom lip), "I let go of expectations of myself and others".

7th (cross the chest to the opposite side and tap under that collar bone), "I allow myself to love myself and others."

8th (lift the non-dominant arm and tap under it on the ribs), "I am love personified."

and 9th (on top of the head), and state, "Even though I sometimes feel… (name that emotion), I still love and appreciate myself.

Tapping Step Three:

Rate the original emotional intensity and repeat if necessary.

You don't have to use my wording. I offer it as a template. There are many others on the internet. Put tapping in the search engine and look.

A couple of things to remember are:

- Use positive language only. Your brain doesn't hear the negatives, so "don't worry" becomes "worry".
- Your brain will experience this as happening NOW. There is no past or future.
- The emotion is the connection between the thought and the belief. You are reprogramming your brain much as you would a computer.
- Tap as much as you need to bring the emotional intensity down to a 1 or 2 out of 10. Be sure to rate the intensity of the emotion prior to tapping on it and immediately afterward.
- Develop your own mantra that fits the emotion you have generated by the thought about a person or event that was distressing to you.

STEP THREE: Create the life you want.

Dream big and do it often. Let yourself feel the emotion of the experience of having what you want. Feel it, see it, hear it, taste it, live it in your mind with such depth that you actually experience it. Don't think about how to get what you want. Allow yourself to just be in the moment of having it as your reality.

Be non-judgmental. By definition, judgement requires appraisal, which requires meaning. Meaning is the result of fitting something into a belief system. If you find yourself evaluating something in this process, "goodness or badness", "rightness or wrongness", you are still functioning within your system of your core beliefs, and that may impede the process of manifesting clearly what you want.

That's it.

DAILY STEPS:

- Take time to be grateful. Do it several times a day until you are living in gratitude all the time.

    o Look at the beauty around you. Take credit for creating it.

    o Think about all the people and things in your life that you experience and be thankful for them. Even the ones that are uncomfortable or painful.

    o Say thank you out loud. Just send thanks outward and don't worry about defining who or what you are sending it to. The experience of gratitude is what you are after.

- Meditate.
    o Turn everything you do into a meditation. When you walk, meditate. When you are cleaning your house, realize you are caring for your creation and let it become a meditation. Let yourself love even the hard to love things. When you see a bug or spider, acknowledge that it is as significant a manifestation as you that is a manifestation of consciousness, a part of your consciousness.

    o There is no right or wrong way to meditate. You can sit in a specific position and intonate a mantra, or you can take a walk. Again, a little research into the subject will yield a plethora of suggestions and ideas.

    o Read or view material that allows your consciousness to expand. Get into the feelings and let yourself go.

Afterthought

The process for manifesting deliberately is ongoing. And it is challenging. But the alternative is to present ourselves time after exhausting and painful time with the same lesson that is designed to move us into authentic alignment with our higher selves.

Learn it or don't. That is the choice we all face. The details become unimportant once the individual has exited their story. They no longer have an emotional impact. The story, the personal history, has lost its power. Do this and you become free to just BE.

I hope this is helpful to anyone who is also on a quest for answers. If I know anything, it is that what we often consider to be truth is nothing more than fiction. And knowing this makes nothing the truth. It's all just creativity for the sake of experience.

My hope is that everyone can become a conscious manifest-master of experience. Just think about the possibilities.

My favorite song is Imagine, by John Lennon (1988). Imagine your life the way you want to have it as much and as often as you can. Dream it. Feel it. Manifest it. In changing your story, you are changing the world. And you are not the only one.

Definitions

MINDFULNESS

- ❖ The practice of maintaining a nonjudgmental state of heightened or complete awareness of one's thoughts, emotions, or experiences on a moment-to-moment basis. --*https://www.merriam-webster.com/dictionary*

- ❖ Mindfulness is a state of active, open attention on the present. When you're mindful, you observe your thoughts and feelings from a distance, without judging them good or bad. Instead of letting your life pass you by, mindfulness means living in the moment and awakening to experience. --Barbara Markway Ph.D.

www.ingramcontent.com/pod-product-compliance
Lightning Source LLC
LaVergne TN
LVHW041811060526
838201LV00046B/1211